AF251321

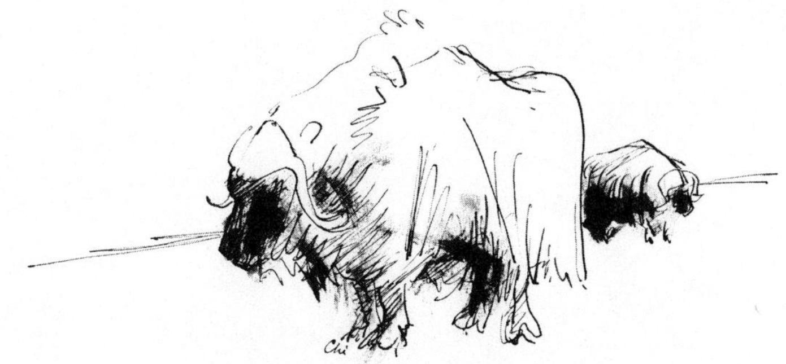

The "Hairy One"

TO STALK THE OOMINGMAK

...*An Artist's Arctic Journal*

Chris Czajkowski

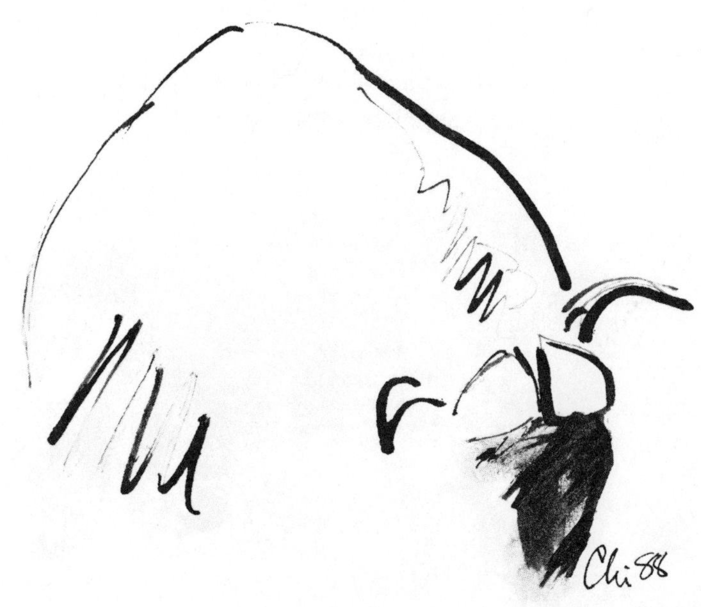

FIRST EDITION

Library of Congress Catalog Card Number: 89-085389
ISBN: 0-9616679-1-5

Published by
Aquarelle Press
P.O. Box 3676
Baton Rouge, Louisiana 70821

Printed by
Printing Incorporated
3019 Plank Road
Baton Rouge, Louisiana 70805

Type face: Zaph International

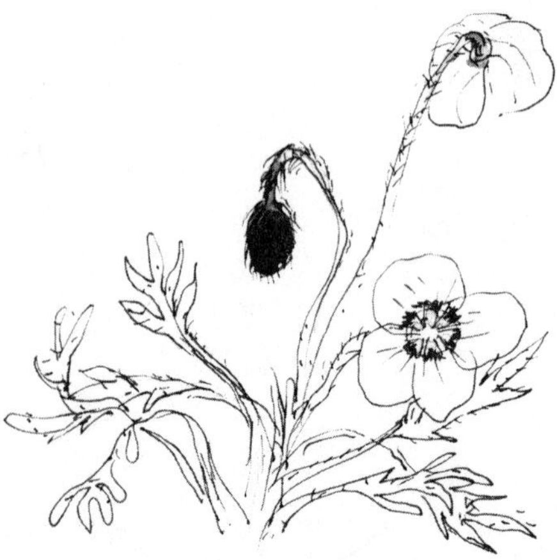

Jacket paintings are original water colors of the Arctic landscape
painted on location by the author. Size 22 x 30 inches

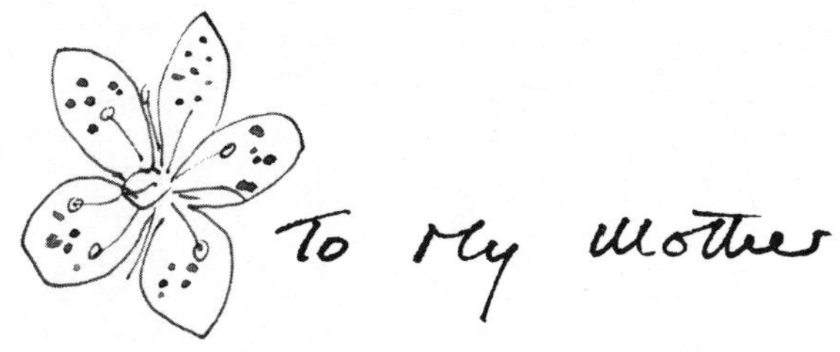

To My Mother

Many years ago, you gave me a present
And I turned the long, slim box in my fingers & said,
"It's not a book."
And you said,
"It might be, one day."
It was a pen.

Countless pens, two typewriters, & a word processor
Later,
Here it is.

Chris

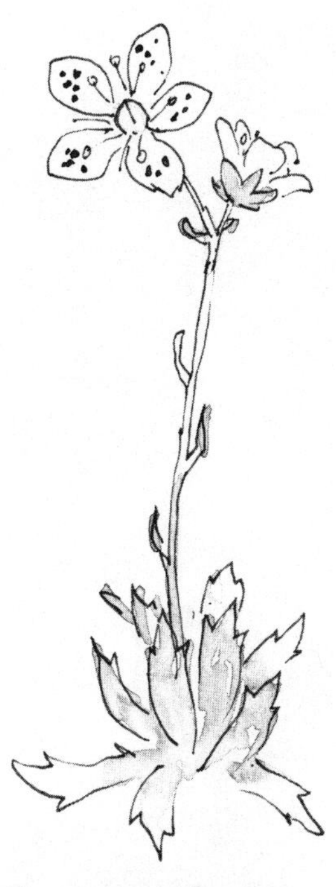

ACKNOWLEDGEMENTS

The people whose lives have touched this journal number too many to be listed individually; it would require another book to explain how they are all involved. But I would like to thank Pete Growski and CBC Radio for the use of material originally broadcast on "Morningside." Fred Breummer, c/o Optimum Publishing International Inc., 4255 St. Catherine Ste. West, Montreal, Quebec, for the use of the two quotations from the native people, which appeared in Mr. Breummer's "*The Arctic*," Katie Hayhurst and Dennis Kuch who have long been the cornerstone to my wilderness.

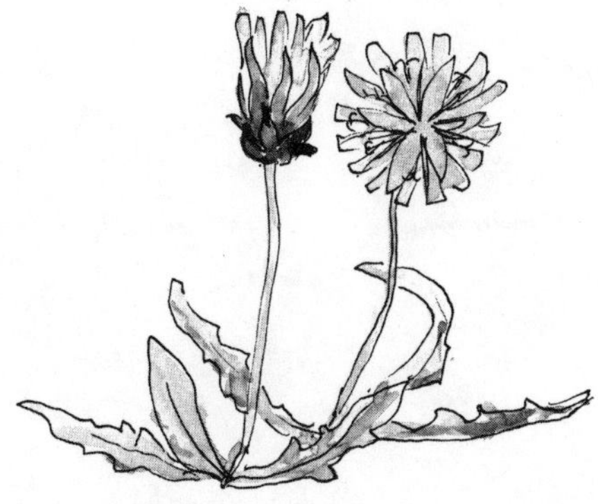

Taraxum hyparcticum

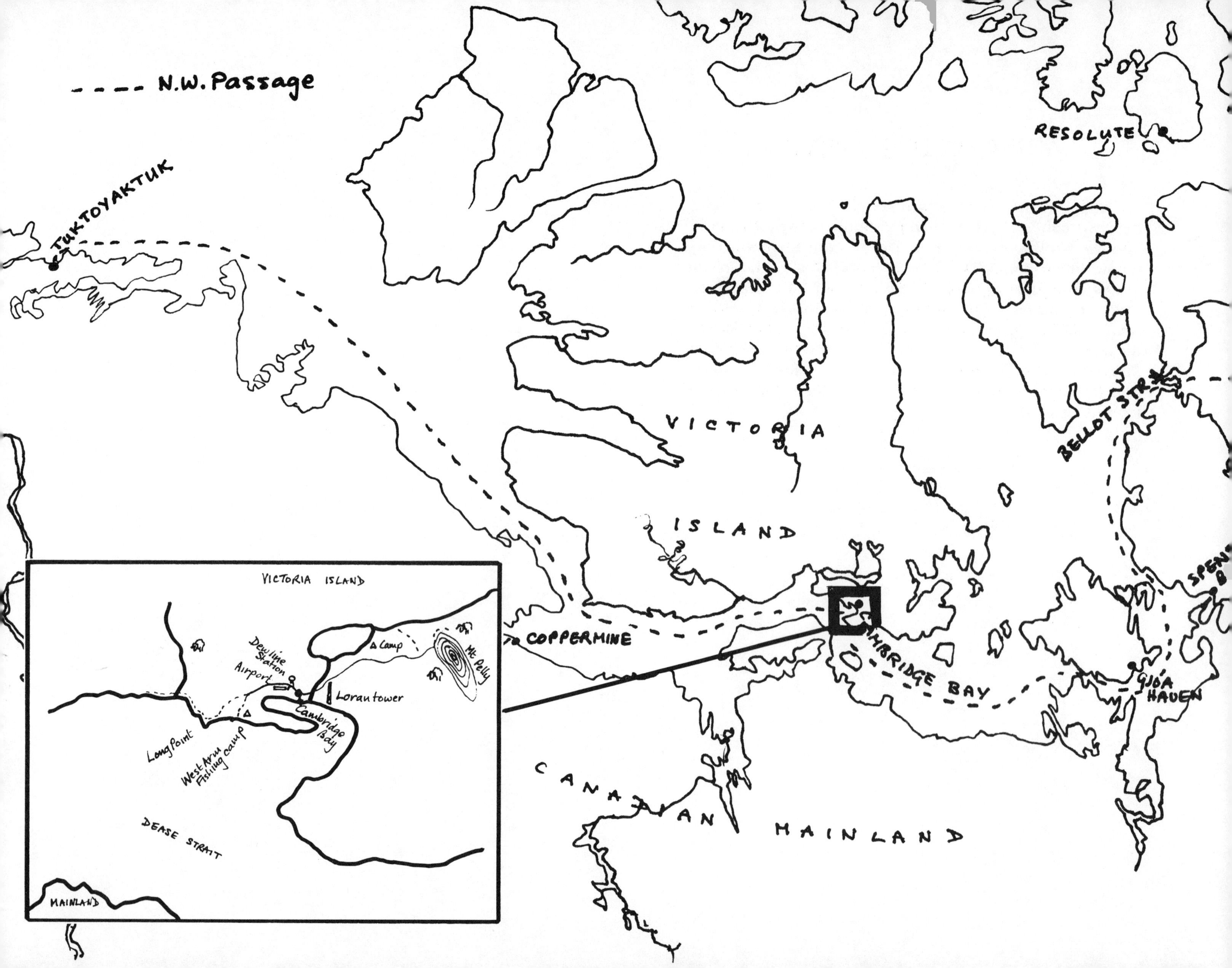
N.W. Passage
TUKTOYAKTUK
RESOLUTE
VICTORIA ISLAND
BELLOT STR.
COPPERMINE
CAMBRIDGE BAY
SPENCE B
GJOA HAVEN
CANADIAN MAINLAND
VICTORIA ISLAND
Dewline Station
Airport
Camp
Mt. Pelly
Loran tower
Cambridge Bay
Long Point
West Arm Fishing camp
DEASE STRAIT
MAINLAND

INTRODUCTION

Have you ever had your portrait painted? Or your photograph taken? Have you ever said (probably politely, under your breath), "That's not a good likeness. That's not really me!"

Of course it's not you — at least, not the way you see yourself. You look at yourself from the inside. And I, no matter how well or little I know you, will see you differently, for I look at you from the outside.

The people who live in the North are constantly being portrayed by writers and photographers. There is a stream of summer people from the South doing research on the plants, the wildlife, the rocks, the weather and The People themselves. There is a well worn saying that an Inuit family (Inuit means The People) consists of mother, father, three kids and an anthropologist. Most of the residents are tired of what they call "being analyzed" and, for that reason, the names of many of those referred to in my journal are false.

The people are real enough, though. To them, their lives are not unusual. Most of the residents were born there, and although many of the rest come for the money then go, some are hooked, and they stay. Often they marry into Inuit families. There is no great fanfare about their decision to stay. They have simply found a way of life that suits their temperament. It would be difficult for them to define their reasons for being there. Rather, they cannot see why they should not.

I can empathize with the people of the Arctic when they tire of the comments of outsiders. My own life seems odd to many, and it puzzles me as to why they should think so. I have built two log cabins, the second single handedly, in wild and rugged locations many miles from the nearest road and neighbour. Why should that seem so strange? I simply prefer to do things my way. I have no trouble at all with the idea that other people's choices are different from mine.

Some call me isolated. But from what am I isolated? I fit my mind and body into rhythms demanded by the weather and the seasons. I am involved with my shelter, my food supply and the stimulation of my mind.

People even call me brave. That is rubbish. It would take much more courage for me to pursue a five day a week existence in a town or city, where I have never lived, than to do what I do in an environment in which I am at home.

I have loved, and lived in wild places in many parts of the world. I grew up in England, moved to East Africa, Australia, New Zealand, the Falkland Islands and now live in Canada. It was inevitable that I should be drawn to the Arctic. I went with no purpose other than curiosity. I wanted to see, hear, taste, and feel something of the wild, windscoured roof of the world. My soul needs the drama of great wilderness.

And despite what I have said, I make no apology for producing yet another book about the Arctic. It is not intended to be a blow by blow account of the way the Arctic eats and thinks and why. It is simply an artist's journal, the account of my experiences, seen through my eyes. And the writing of it, and the drawing of it, was as necessary to me as breathing.

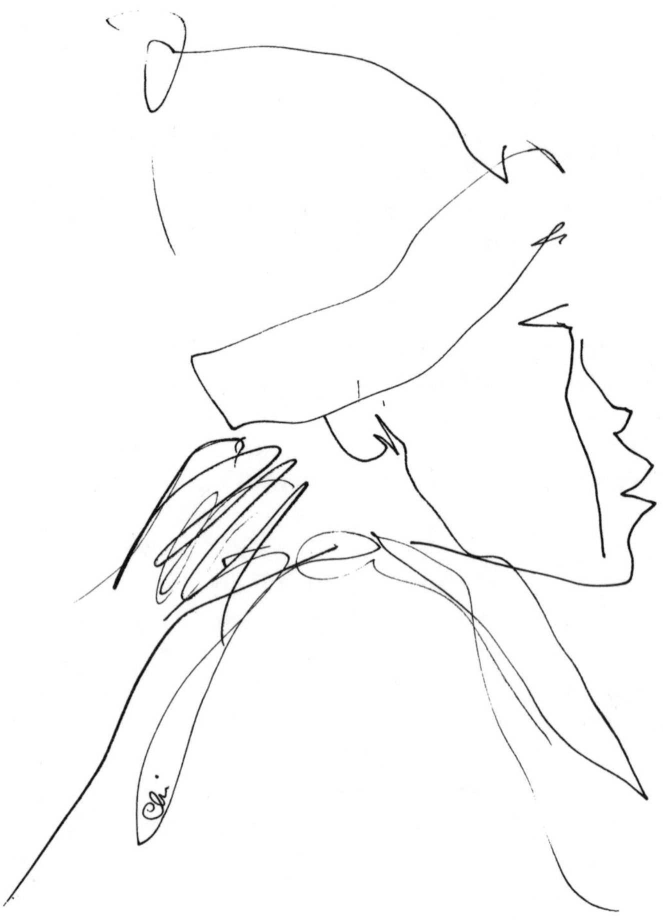

My Father, you have spoken well;
You have told me that Heaven is very beautiful
Tell me one more thing.
Is it more beautiful than the country of the
*   muskox in summer.*
Where sometimes the mist
Blows over the lakes,
And sometimes the water is blue,
And the loons cry very often?

Saltatha, Warburton Pikes's Indian guide talking to a priest.

28th June

The town is not an attractive place on first acquaintance. The unit, which I am temporarily inhabiting while the owner is away, is superheated and provided with every convenience, but the walls are thin, and the neighbours shake the rooms with their movements. The buildings across the street, a mirror to these, are squat and utilitarian with small, blind, triple-sealed windows, multihued, but faced with ticky tacky and faded under the overcast sky which dominates at this time of year. There are no yards. Rickety wooden steps lead from each door to the whitish, mud-coloured road, which is lined with bits of snow-machines, rusty oil drums, garbage, and chained dogs. The buzz of balloon-tyred trikes is continuous, for in this place, which needs only five minutes to walk from one end to the other, everyone drives.

Friends of mine, Katie and Dennis, are working here for a couple of years. This house is two doors down from theirs, and I am grateful for it, for I could never have afforded to come here otherwise. The only hotel, a vast, creaking wooden structure, like something out of the gold rush days, costs $100 a day, $150 with food. Even so, it is always full. Katie tells me that when she visits other settle-

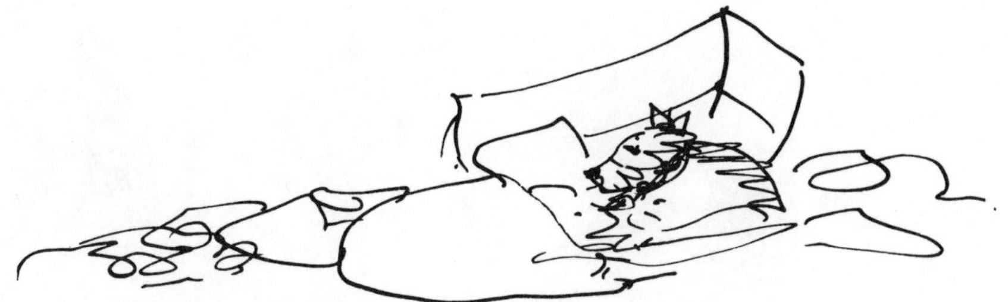

ments as part of her job, she often has to share a room, sometimes with the cook.

The regular occupant of my unit is a teacher. She is away for the school vacation. A photograph of a blond boy about two years old adorns one of the walls, and the house is full of his possessions. The mother obviously loves the child, but she must be very firm with him, for the place is achingly clean and excruciatingly tidy. The boy's imaginative art work is taped in exact rows above his meticulously parked trucks, and in the porch, on the shelf above the freezer, gloves and mitts are placed one above the other, thumb to thumb and finger to finger.

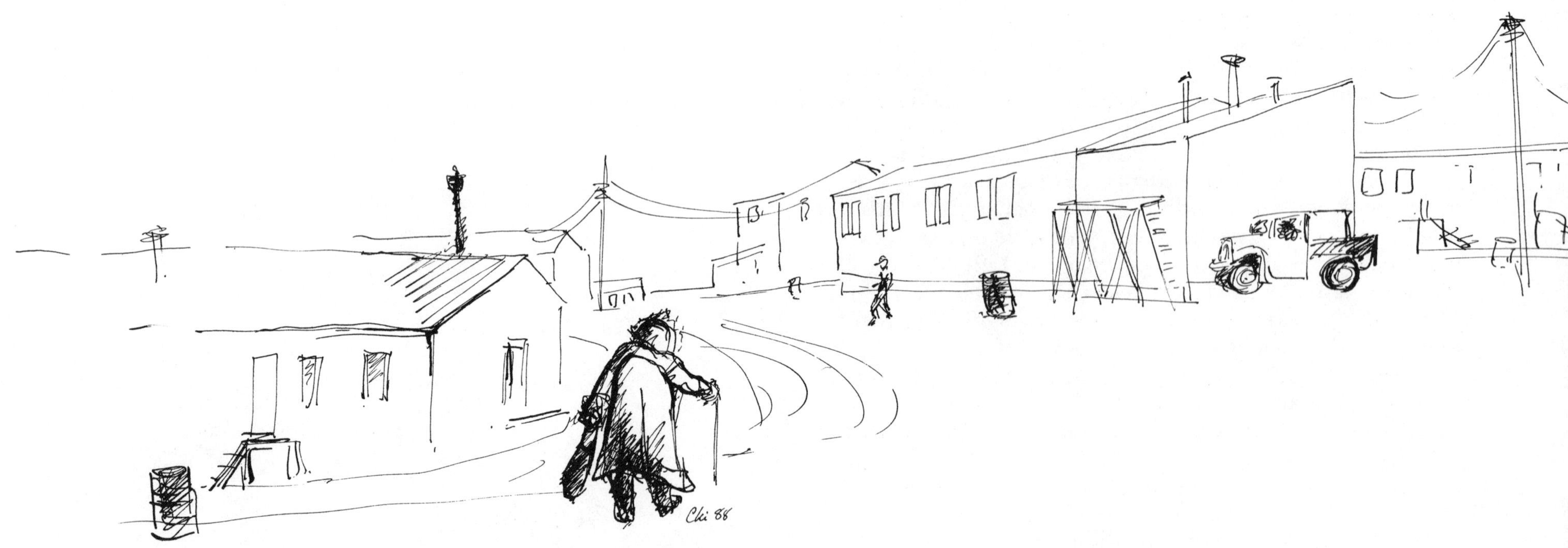

In the superheated atmosphere, hothouse plants thrive; waxy, exotically marked leaves, and gaudy, plastic-looking flowers. They are a direct contrast to the dreariness beyond the window. Wind whines in throbbing power-lines: people bow before it, muffled, mittened, zippered to the chin. I had expected space when I came to the Arctic, but the town is cramped, for in winter, a journey of even a few yards may become a major expedition. "It wouldn't be so bad if it wasn't for the wind," says Katie. "At -40°C, the chill factor may be -80°C. The fur on the hoods of our parkas makes a tunnel round our faces, but even so, our noses become frost-bitten. You have no idea how strange it is to push the hood back, now it is summer, and be able to see all around. It is almost frightening, like taking the blinders off a horse, so that unexpected shapes and move-ments come at you from the side. Everything looks so strange without the snow, too. I haven't got used to it yet. Two weeks ago, we were still using snow machines."

Two weeks ago. That was mid-June. Katie and Dennis have a seven year old boy. He hates it here, when he thinks about it. He frequently walks backwards home from school when he cannot face the wind.

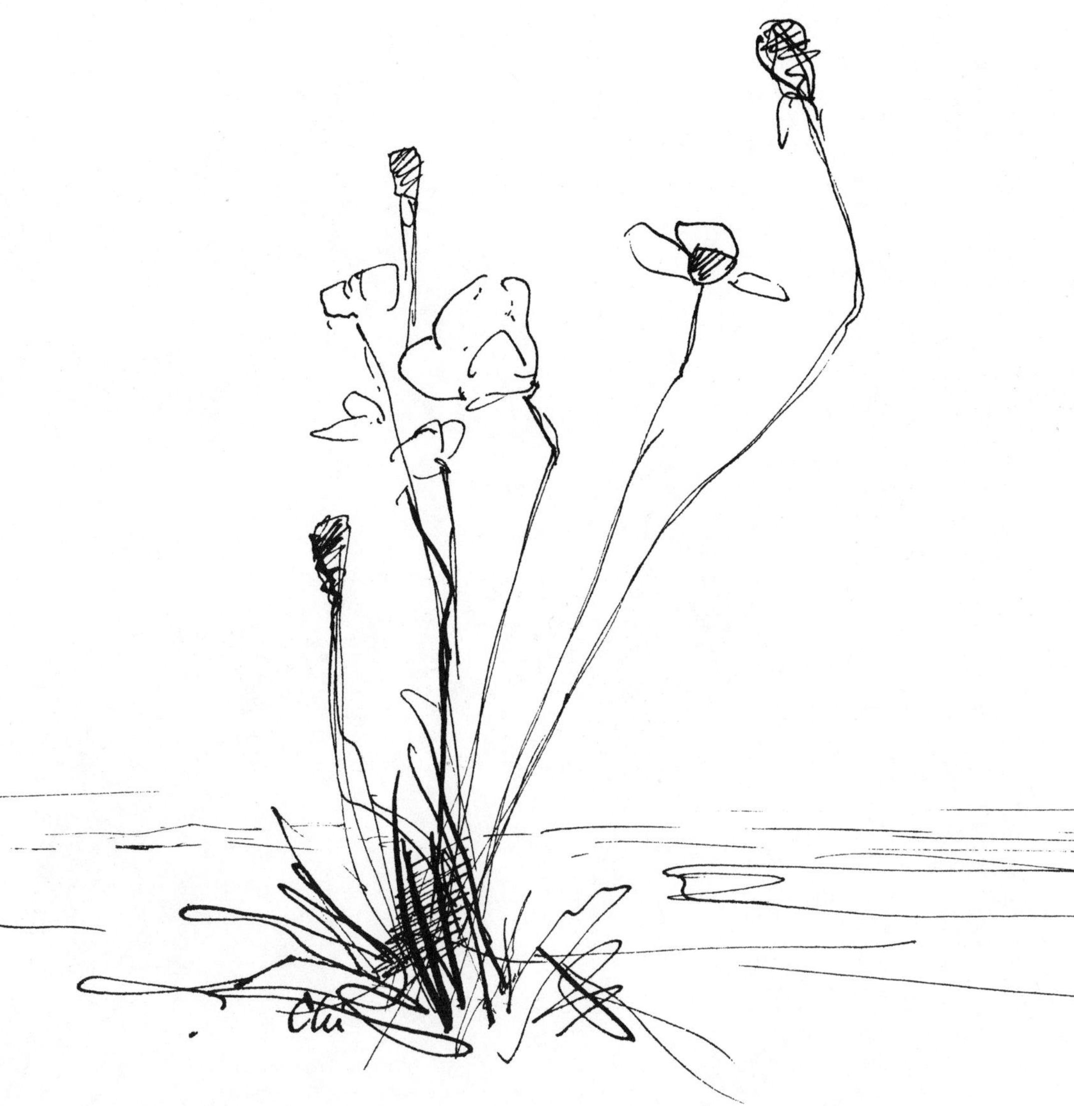

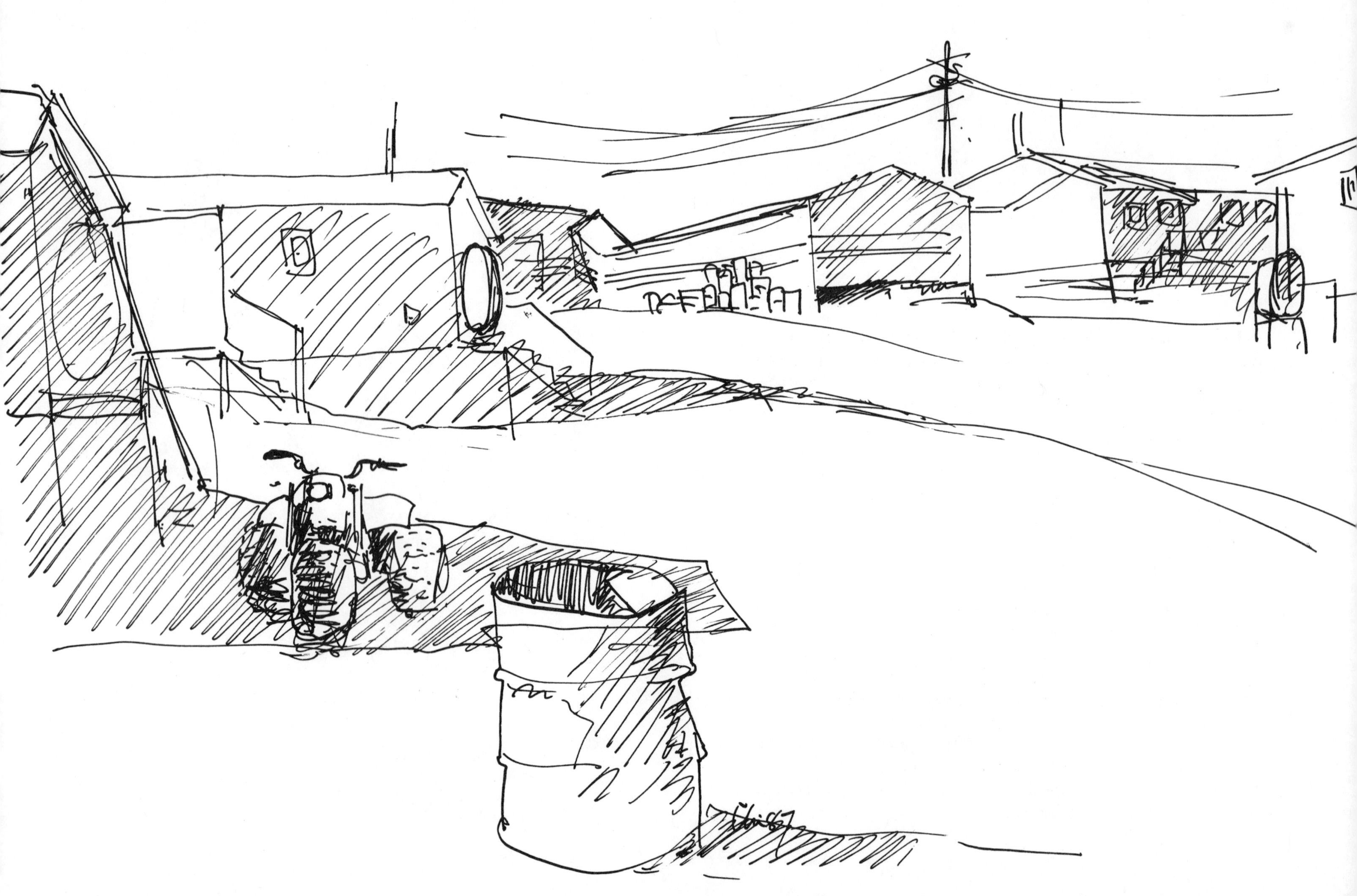

On my second evening, a group of us went towards Mt. Pelly, a long slab of a hill, slightly humped, like a whale, a few hundred feet higher than the rest of the tundra. We were to leave after work, but time slides easily in a land of eternal day, and it was more like 9 P.M. before we set off, five adults and two kids, bulkily clothed and helmeted, on three balloon-tyred trikes. The kids rode up on the gas tanks, and I rode on the back carrier behind one of Katie's office contemporaries. This manipulator of governmental statistics was a young, garrulous fellow who delighted in seeking the slitheriest mud and roughest bumps on the tundra when deep bog holes forced us off the narrow, gravel road.

Tundra. The very word evoked a sense of space, distance, loneliness. A land where the elements ruled, in which man, soft bodied, insect puny, had little business. Like a snail, he must drag his shell of technology with him to survive. From between the puny verticals of town, the harsh, thin, horizontal slab of grey brown land had looked frighteningly empty, and I had savoured the thought of this, my first expedition onto it, with awe. But, careening along in my too tight helmet, cocooned in noise and protective clothing, I could grasp little of the tundra. The vignettes that flew past my retina were empty of sound or smell or feeling. Twice, we crossed small rivers, clear, and not very deep, but swift enough to pile against us on the upstream sides and flood our boots. The balloon tyres made the vehicle want to float away. At every bump our carapaced heads bonked together. Somewhere to the north, hidden in cloud, was the sun.

We stopped at last by a piece of water, and I unclamped my mittened fingers from the trike's carrier. We were beside a large lake, but as most of it was covered with ice, and much of the land out here still retained scalloped drifts of snow, it was difficult to see where tundra ended and water began. My companion had expostulated at length about all the fish we were bound to catch, and at his urging, I had gone to the store to buy line and lures and a five dollar license, and spent time cutting a broken hockey stick into lengths to make jigging sticks. But there was dismay when it was discovered that meltwater now lay between us and the ice, sufficient to prevent us crossing onto it, and jigging was no longer possible. Two of the men had rods, and they cast happily and fruitlessly for awhile into the lake, but the water was shallow and they hooked only stones.

We were by no means the only townsfolk out here. Vehicles buzzed and rattled continuously up and down the road, and nearby, a family of Inuit was camping in a faded, heavy canvas tent stretched over a frame of two-by-fours. The people love to go onto the land in summer, and the tents spring up, even on waste lots close to town, the moment the ground appears through the snow. This family had a fire of broken packing cases on which they were roasting wieners. A rack, built out of reach of dogs, held two red-fleshed char and a blotched lake trout, and some curled slabs of dried cariboo meat as dark and brittle as old boot leather. A garbage bag flapped and jerked above them in an attempt to deter gulls and ravens.

The Inuit offered us tea, and we warmed our hands around hot tin mugs, and nibbled chunks of crispy bannock. There were grannies and babies and all ages in between. We asked them about the fishing, and how long they had been there. "About 10 days," they said, "and the fishing has been poor this year. The spring run is late, for there is too much ice in the river, and now the water has melted at the edge of the lake, we cannot get out on the ice. The fishing would have been much better there."

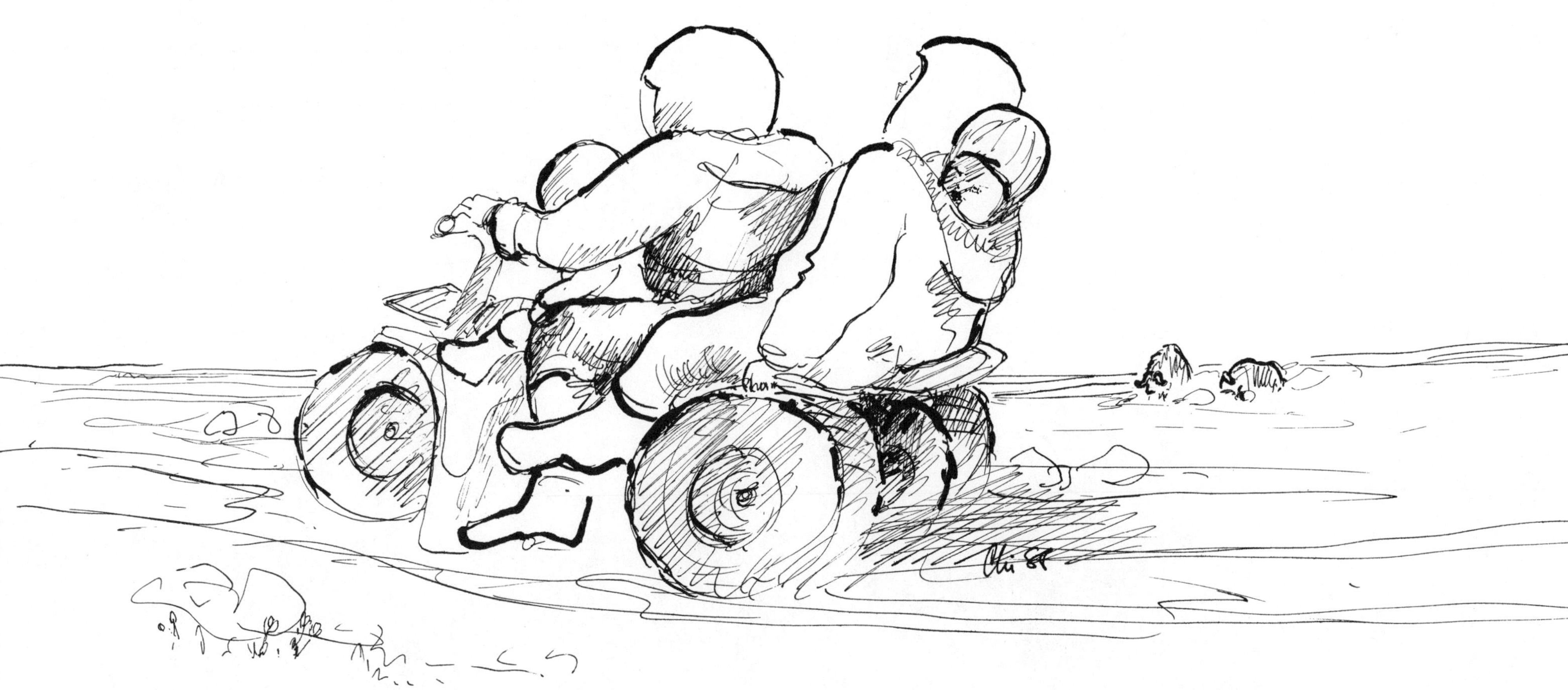

A young man asked us if we wanted to see some muskox—Oomingmak, he called them. A herd had been spotted on the far side of the mountain, and if we hurried, we might catch them. So we took our leave: "Thank you for the tea."

"Thank you for visiting us," said granny. We jammed on the helmets and crammed onto the trikes and slewed and slithered to the base of the mountain. We were stopped by a snowdrift, and we abandoned the vehicles and began to climb. The racket of machines dropped behind and, at last, with the measured tread of boot on rock, the tundra grew in depth and definition. These were curious rocks which held our feet, flat and platelike, yellowish, and heavily blotched with black and orange lichen. They cracked and clinked as we walked. Between them grew dense, sprawling, stalkless cushions of an intensely rich and lusciously purple saxifrage, which blooms profusely, like the Inuit tents, the moment the snow departs.

This was the highest land for miles around. To the north, the heavy cloud layer, separated from the earth like the sky

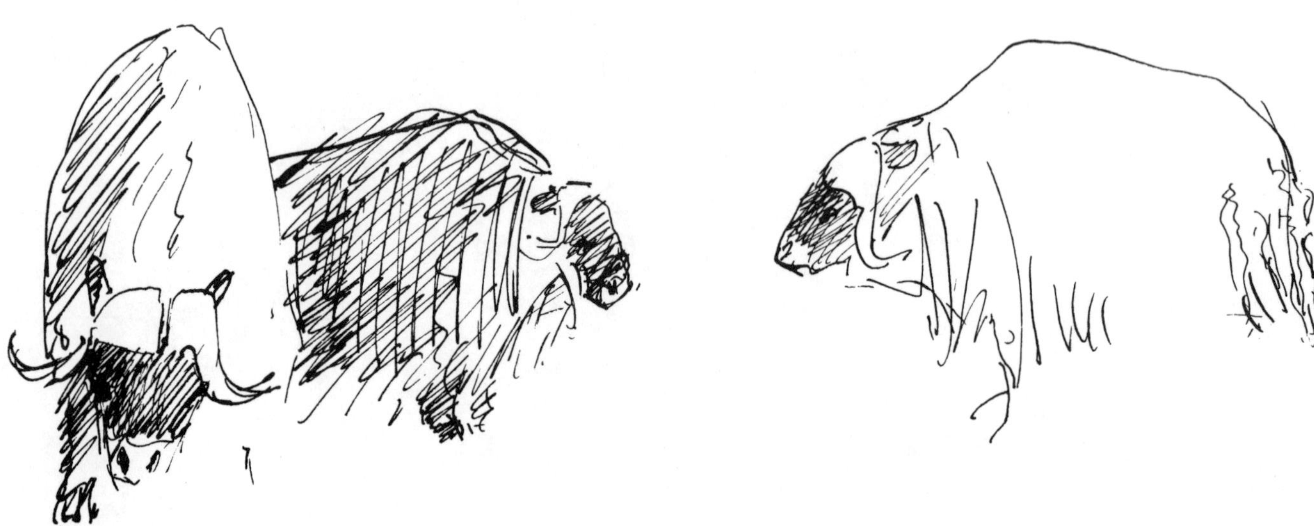

in a child's drawing, roofed a horizontal slab of sullen
orange, all we saw of the sun that night, although it will
continue to revolve around the sky until sometime in August. It was raining a little. Pooled within the snow-
streaked web of ridge and bog, melting ice stretched far
into the misty distance, all pale greens and greys and
turquoises.

"It's midnight," said Dennis, but it didn't feel it. No one
was tired, not even the kids, but they, now that school was
out, would sleep till noon and beyond the following day.

We surprised the muskox in a hollow, thirteen of them,
two of them calves. They did not like us and ran away,
loosely bunched, their long skirts swaying like bustles, and
rags of down flying off them like spray. We ran behind and
plucked the down off the tundra, the warmest, lightest
fibre in the world, soft, like a cloud. The muskox stopped
and looked at us, long coats blowing, primeval in the dull
light of the arctic summer night.

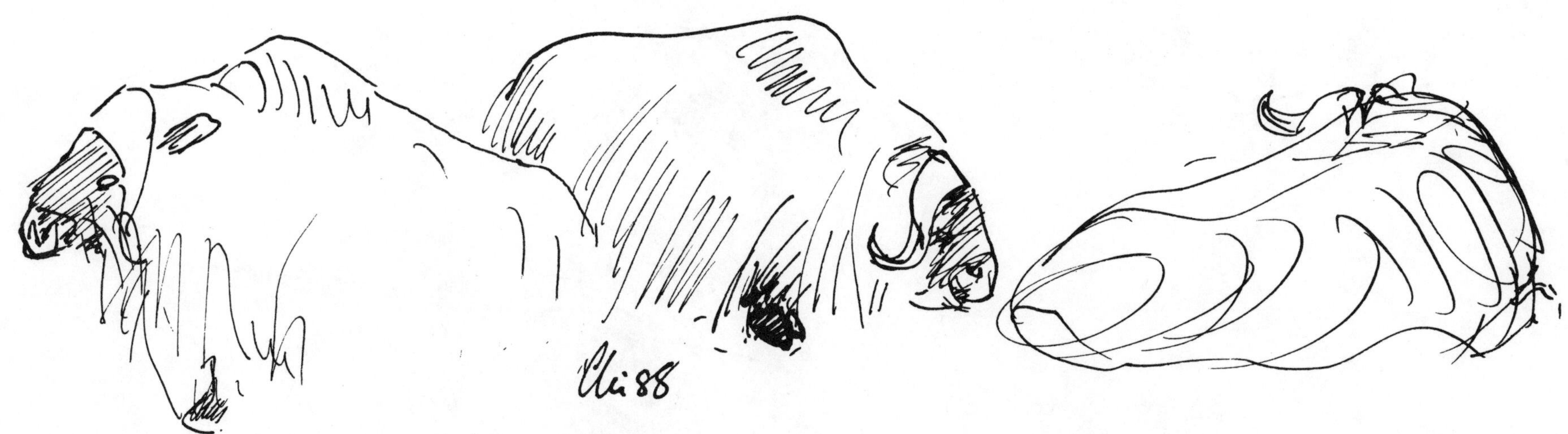

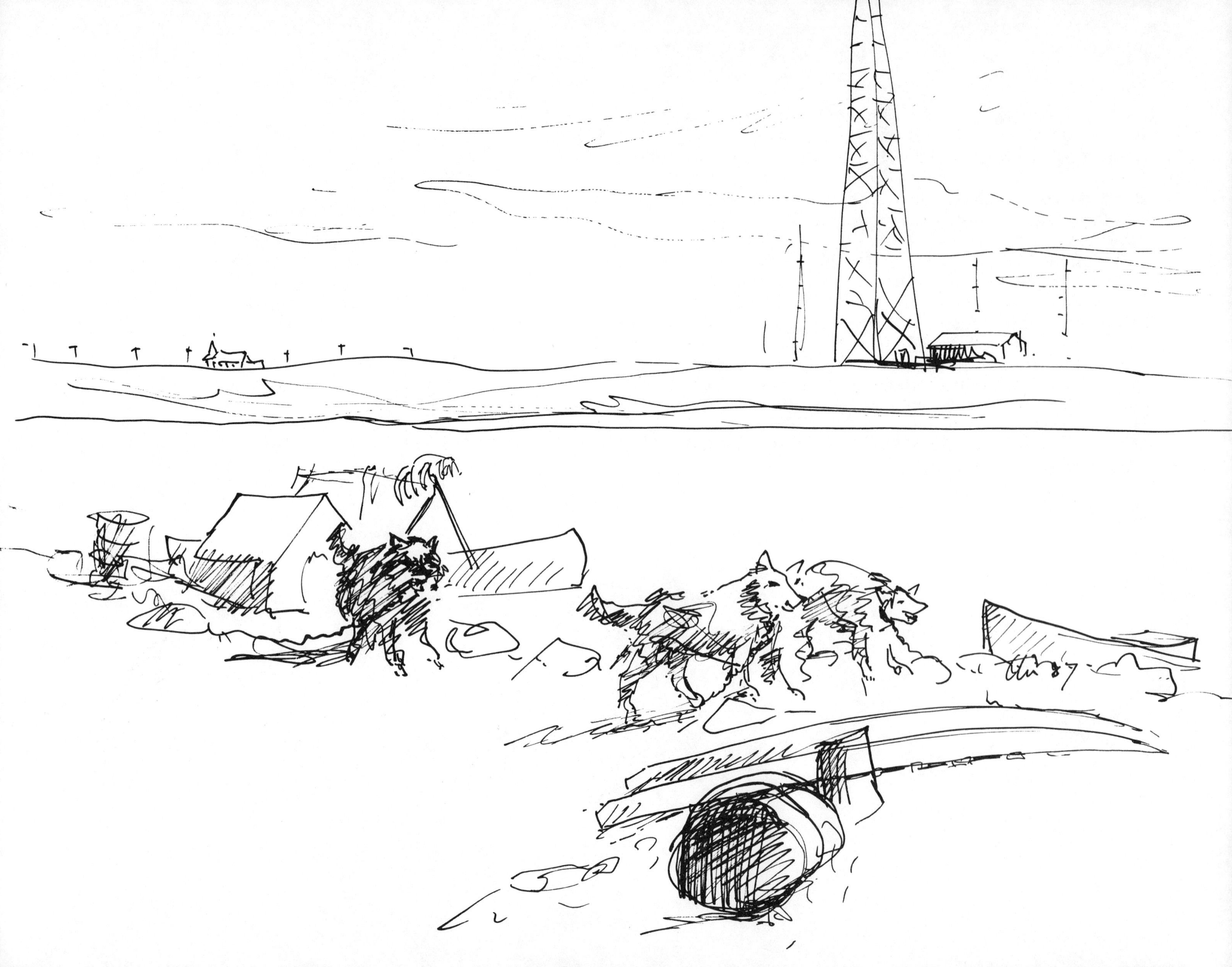

The sea, which curves around the town, is frozen six feet deep, but it is pooled with water and split with green gloomy canyons, in one of which a child drowned just before I arrived. The people nudge their snowmachines and komatiks out to sea in pursuit of fish or seals, but they must use boats to cross the strip of water by the shore. The waterfront is an incredible collection of junk, battered oil drums, broken packing cases, plastic, crazily parked boats, and more dogs, which lie, pale as stones, among the boulders. They leap and lunge ferociously, heavy chains dragging, if anyone comes too close. At this time of year, they have little else to do. At noon and 10 P.M. a siren wails, and all the dogs howl in unison. Beyond their worn circles of bones and beaten earth, tiny flowers are beginning to bloom, unravaged by the passage of traffic, guarded unwittingly by the ferocity of the dogs.

I have been trying to draw. The wind ripped the first page off my pad before I could touch it, bowling it along the shore among the dogs. I clamped the rest, hurriedly, with bulldog clips, but removing a sheet was very difficult; they all became battered and crumpled before I could store them safely.

This is an odd community. I am used to isolated settlements, for I have always lived in remote areas, but this one

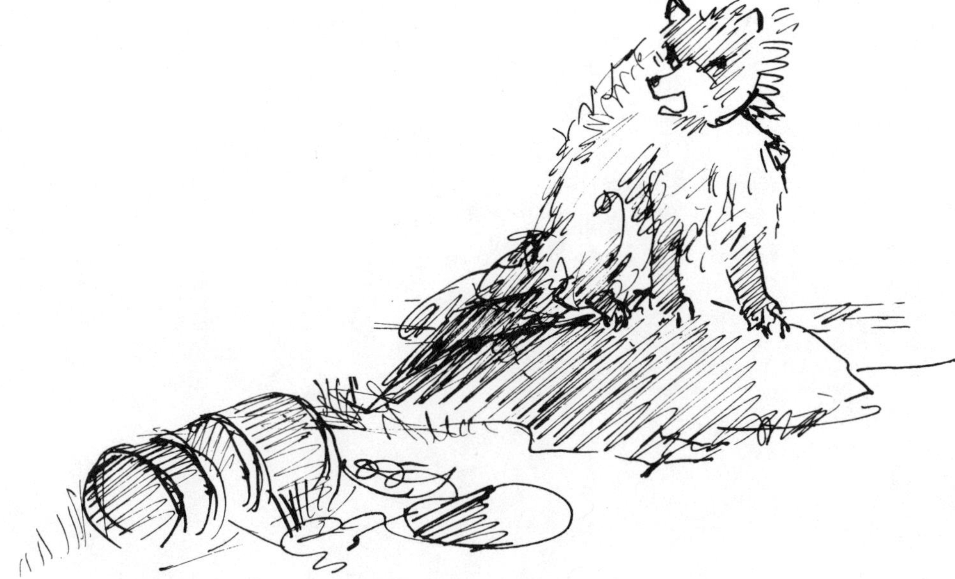

is different. No one knows anyone else. There is no community. There are no clubs, no groups of bird watchers or craftspeople. Only a small clique who get together for alcoholic parties with the residents of the DEW line station beyond the airport. Katie and Dennis have been here six months, but when I mention their names, no one has heard of them. This would be impossible at home.

There are probably several reasons for this. Firstly, most of the population is transient. Most whites come up from the south on two-year contracts, but even the natives are often here only for a few months of training. On the streets, everyone is friendly, in passing. They smile and wave, but all are bundled against the weather and helmeted on bikes, so it is usually impossible to tell to whom you are waving, friend or stranger, native or white. No one stops to gossip, and no one has fences to lean on and chatter with their neighbours. I hear the people move next door and feel the building shake as their outer door slams, but I don't know what any of them look like, except the small boy on my right. He is, at this moment, playing alone in the street, weaving wobbling circles with his bike. He is a native, and his store-bought parka hood is trimmed with white fox fur. Slowly and expertly, he blows a large, pink, bubble of gum.

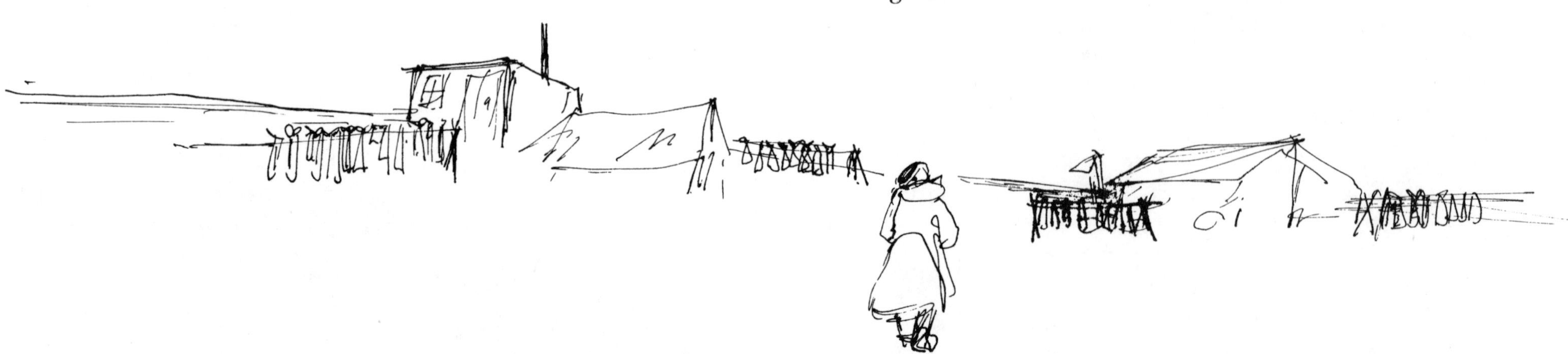

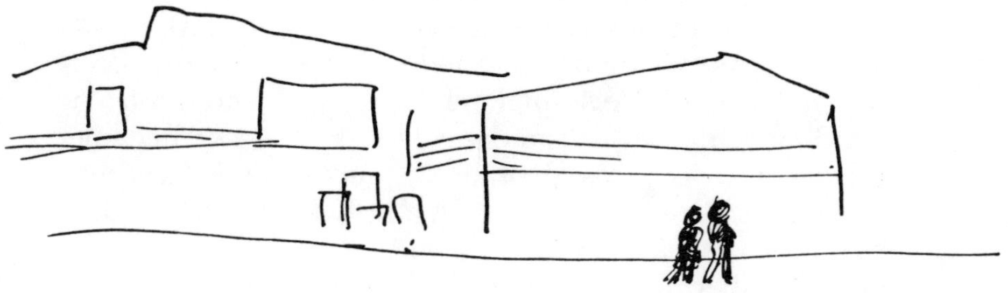

I wanted to bake bread, and as I rummaged about the kitchen for utensils, I could not help but speculate about the regular occupant of this house. Her name is Susan Mackay, for it is printed in round, clear letters, teacher fashion, in a pair of rubber boots on the porch. I could find no bread tins, or even a cutting board or bread knife, but a shiny electric toaster lay on a tray, and the remnants of a cardboard-tasting packet of sliced bread sat in the fridge. Typical city, I thought. I borrowed what I needed from Katie and Dennis. Strangely, the drawer beside the sink was full of meat knives, all very sharp.

Yesterday, I walked beyond the settlement out onto the Mt. Pelly road. The close-packed buildings end abruptly, as if cut off with a knife, but it is difficult to shrug off the town's influences. The road winds upon an esker, a sinuous gravel ridge conveniently deposited by a glacier when the last ice age retreated. About a mile from town, a gravel sorter bellows hideously, and big bulldozers with great buckets feed chunks of esker through its grinding maw. The dump sends aromas, charred paper, and unconsumed styrofoam chips downwind.

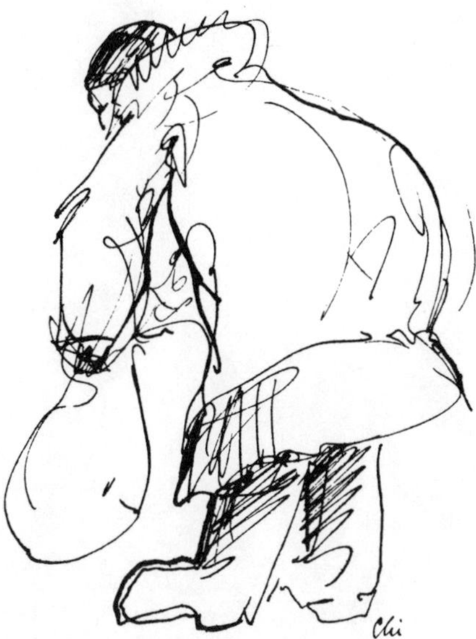

It was a wild day of shrieking winds and clouds like explosions ripped apart on top. Bitter rain dissolved distances or swept against my coat, rattling on the fabric, and beating painfully on unprotected skin. Occasionally, fleeting shafts of intense sunlight shot hot gold onto tundra or blinding white on ice, and meltwater, and sky became, briefly, a vivid tropical blue. Distances were deceptive; close things seemed far, and far things close. Huge white birds flew in a long, low line, and I thought, through the rain, that they must be swans, until I saw their short necks and black capped heads and recognized them for terns. And after some hours, when I seemed to have been fighting the wind for miles, I turned back towards Cambridge Bay, and the township looked only minutes away, a huddle of harsh angles and glittering roofs, with the alien, silvery balls and discs of the DEW line station stuck up upon the tundra close by, like something out of a science fiction story.

Large areas of land seemed grey, barren as a field of rubble, but these, surprisingly, were thickly massed with flowers, fuzzy plumes of the arctic willow, erect and leafless, as densely packed as organ pipes. One must turn one's back on the distances and crawl on hands and knees to really appreciate the tundra. Within the silvery cocoons of the willow blossoms, red and yellow tipped stigmata nestle, like pairs of microscopic horns. Sometimes clouds of pollen blow.

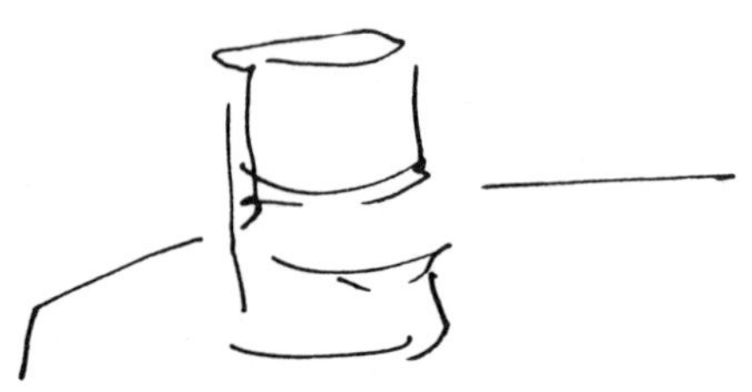

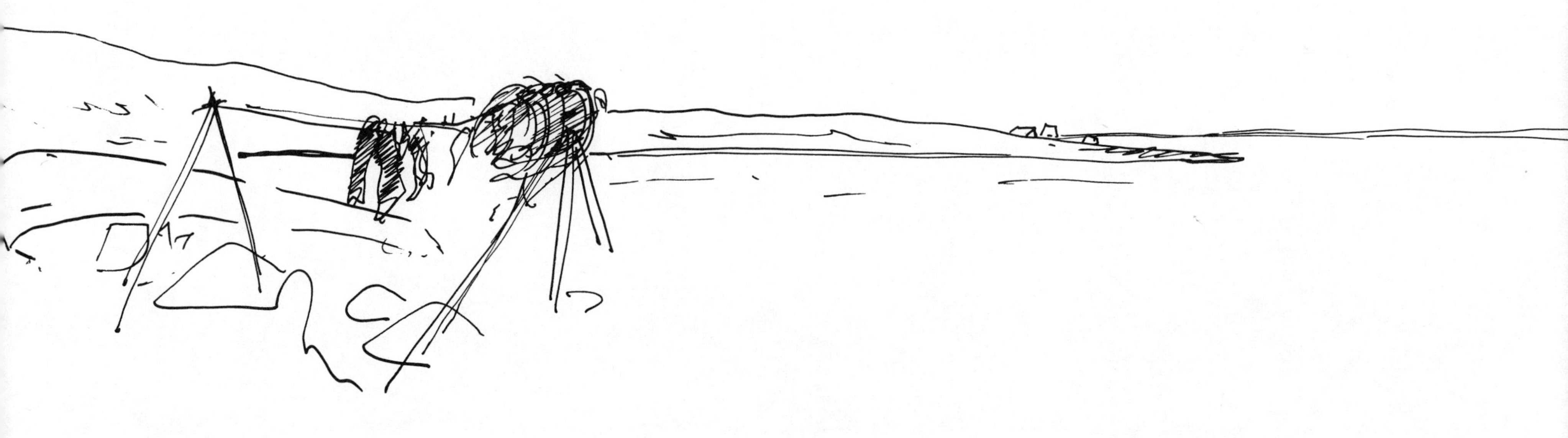

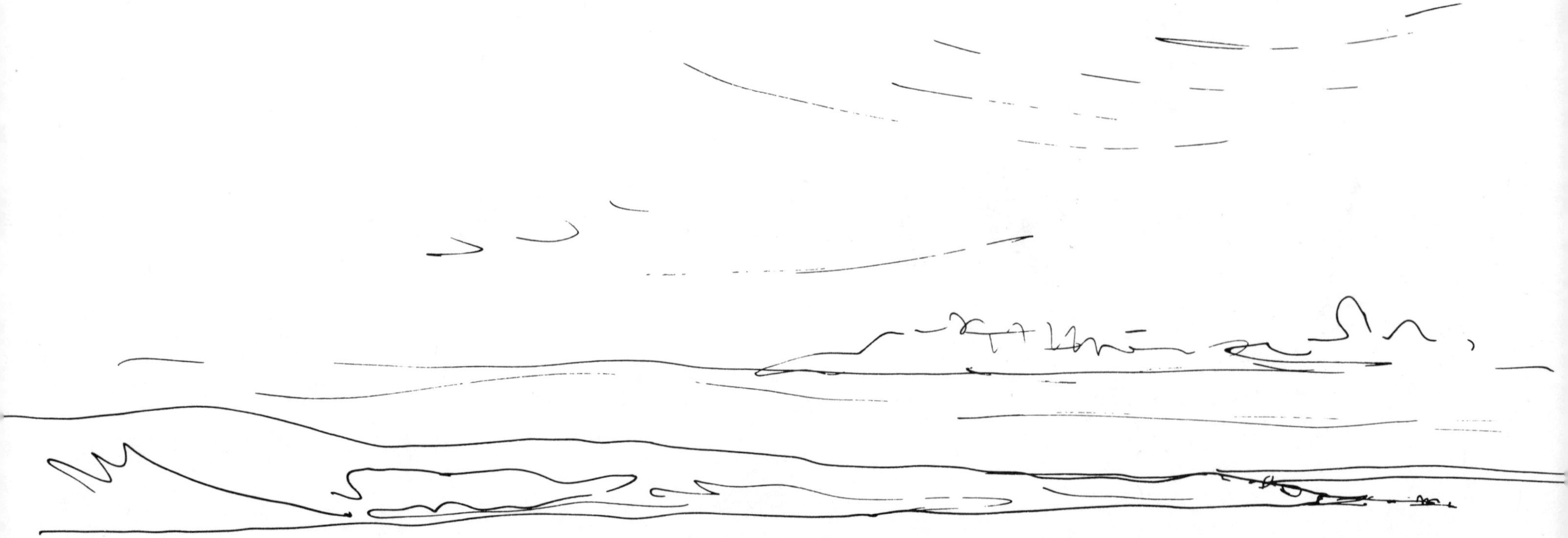

It is midnight, or thereabouts. I have no watch, but the sun is low in the north, and its orange light shines on the far side of the little valley — hardly more than a depression, really — in which I am camped. The tent is in shadow, tucked within the shelter of the valley's rim, but still it creaks and flaps in the eternal wind. It is cold, and I am glad of my down coat and sleeping bag, and I hold the pen between gloved fingers. The door of the tent is tied back as far as it will go, for I am waiting for the fox.

The jaegers will tell me when she appears, for they scream and swoop at any intruder, including others of their own kind who would be just as likely to steal their green, blotched eggs. Sometimes the fox leaps and snaps at them, but mostly she ignores them and lopes swiftly along the full length of the valley, stopping momentarily to sniff a lemming hole or stare sharply, without fear, in my direction. She has a den, a warren of burrows dug into a sandy spur, hidden from the tent by a swell in the land. The ground about it is littered with the remains of meals, feathers, eggshells, and a half rotten cariboo leg filched, no doubt, from the discarded carcasses that lie along the coast. It is when the light begins to mellow and the shadows start to lengthen that the cubs come out to play. There

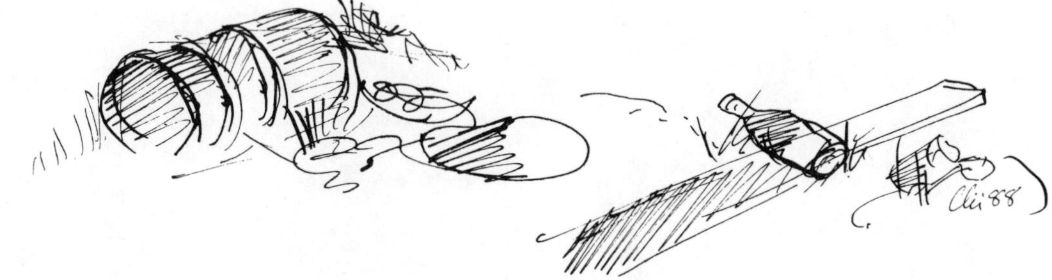

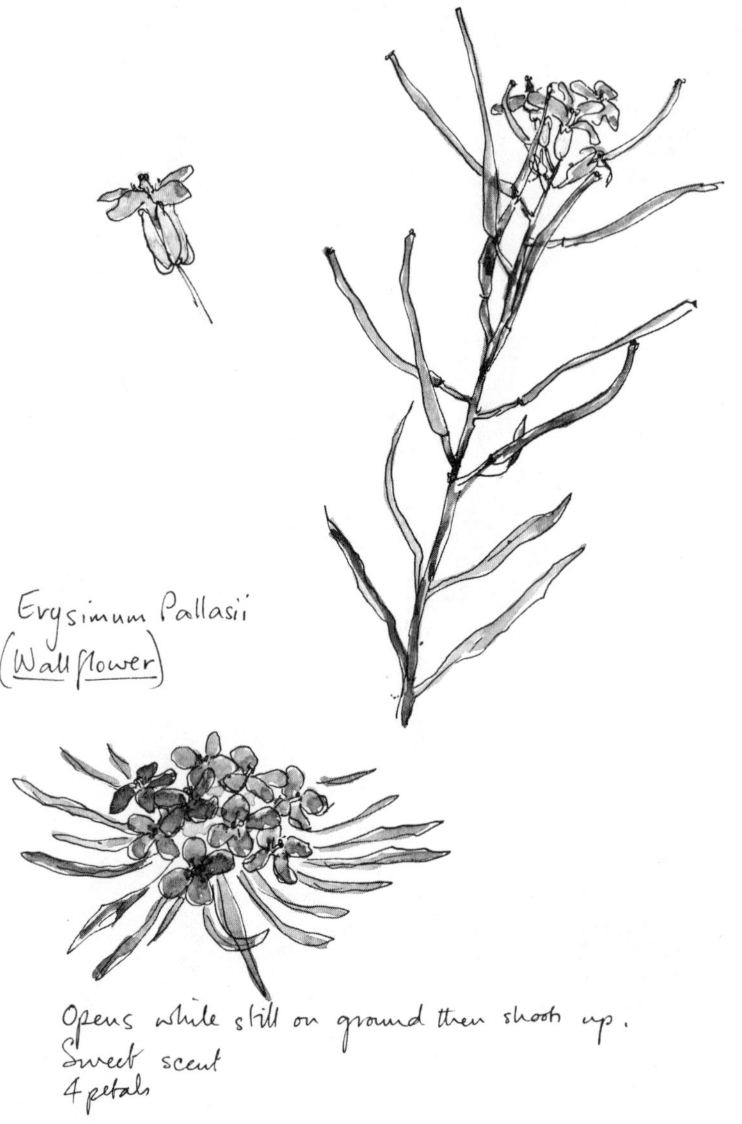

are three of them. They are aware of me long before I can get close enough to see them properly, for there is nowhere to hide in this bald and naked land. Two are simply curious, but the third is timid and gives a hoarse, wheezy bark more like the cry of a bird than a carnivore and, at his warning, they all scuttle down the holes and out of sight. If I am patient and wait in silence, a sharp little nose and a pair of rounded, furry ears will pop up, then down when I am seen, but the cubs will not come out again when I am there. They do well to be cautious, for close by is a leg trap, rusted and half buried in the grass. Perhaps it was a man who brought the cariboo leg.

Katie brought me out here on her trike, borrowing a trailer from a neighbour to carry my gear. I am west of town beyond the airport, at the head of a long, narrow arm of the sea. I can still hear the buzz of ATVs, as people pass along the road to the fishing camp further down the coast, but I cannot be seen by anyone, and I have, at last, a measure of privacy. Most visitors to the Arctic come from cities, and they think Cambridge Bay the peak of isolation. But I live far from neighbours and I find the little town confining; I can never relax surrounded by people.

The weather has been glorious. The sun turns full circle in a cloudless sky. When it travels through the southern half of its journey, the temperature is warm in sheltered corners, but these are few, and the wind still bites through shirts and sweaters, and windproof clothing is needed much of the time. The plants make their own shelter by growing in humped masses and opening their blossoms on the sunny, leeward side. All manner of these have responded to the warmth. There is no time for ceremony. Three weeks ago, it was winter; today, it is summer. A species found in bud one day will be in full bloom the next. One extraordinary-looking plant excited me greatly. It started life as a silvery grey fuzzball the size of an egg, set point up as if sitting in an egg cup. Within the downy fibres, small leaves and buds peeped shyly. The day it opened, brilliant pink candles erupted everywhere. They grew taller as more flowers opened, and some inflorescences reached six or eight inches in height. They are aptly named "woolly lousewort" or "bumblebee plant."

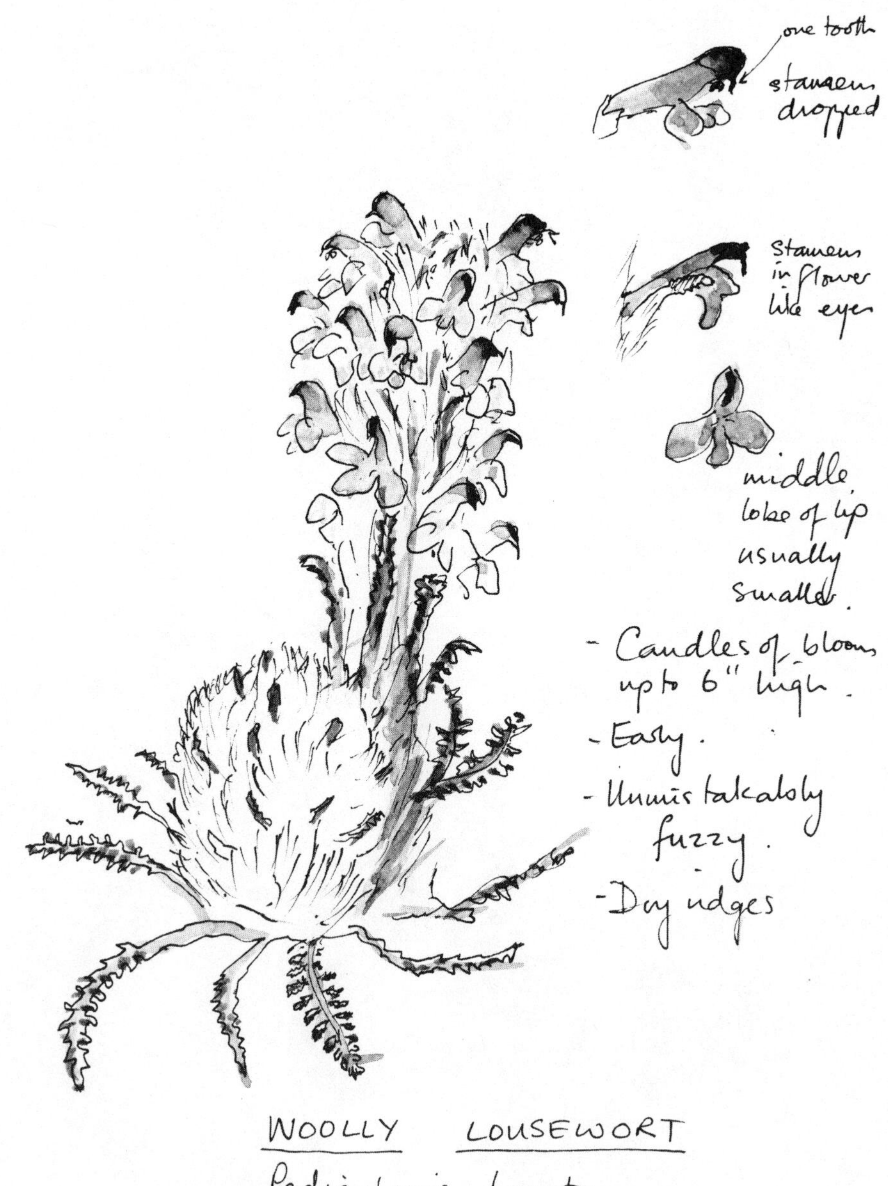

WOOLLY LOUSEWORT
Pedicularis lanata

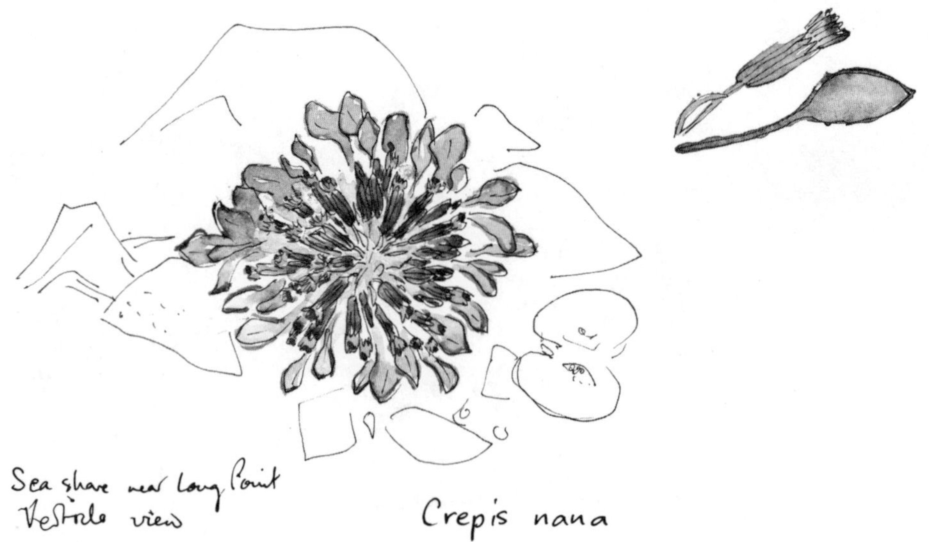

Sea share near Long Point
Vestrile view

Crepis nana

Most of the tundra was well established, a thick, boggy mat of mosses, lichens, liverworts, sedges, and dwarf willow. I crossed these areas sometimes, but they ran with snowmelt, and my leather hiking boots have seen better days and leaked abysmally. In any case, the spongy tussocks made walking difficult. In places, curious extrusions of mud had flowed from beneath the tundra's surface, and lay whitish and cracking in the drying wind, testament to the mysterious forces of thaw. Because of the permafrost, nothing can drain away, and all must be forced up: which is why the ground is swampy and thickly laced with ponds, although the average annual precipitation of ten inches would class the area, in a warmer climate, as a desert.

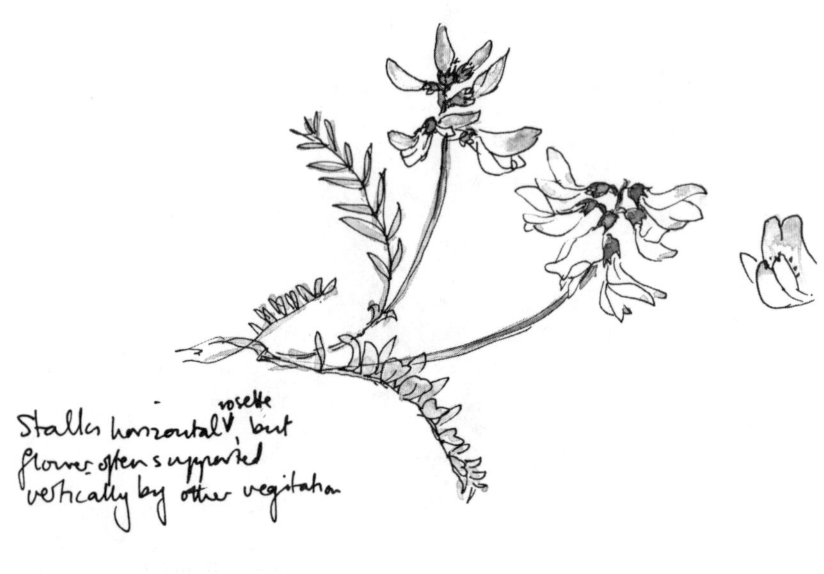

Stalks horizontal, but
flower often supported
vertically by other vegitation

rosette

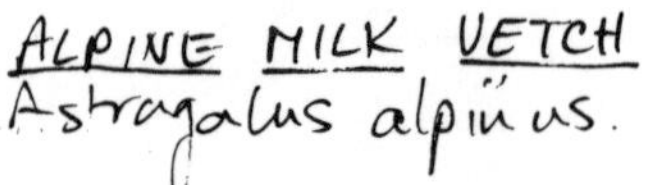

ALPINE MILK VETCH
Astragalus alpinus.

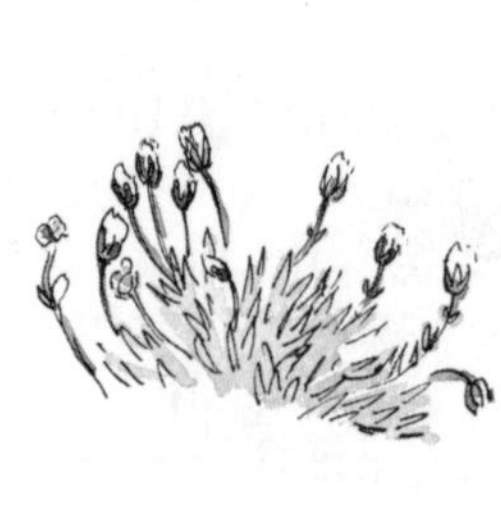

Arenaria rubella

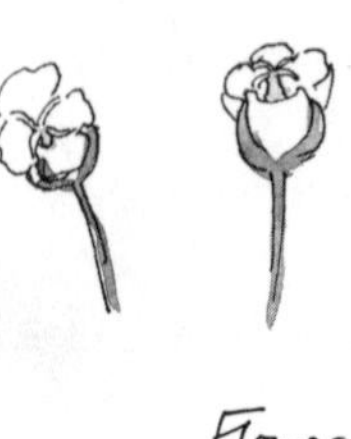

Flower appears to
be divided into
4 sections by.
stigma which
has 4 horns.
4 petals.

But it was the gravel ridges that fascinated me most. Here a multitude of flowering plants delighted the eye, new ones opening every day. There were vetches, saxifrages, avens, daisies, potentillas, and many which I could not identify. I was surprised to find representations of the pea family, for I thought this meant insect pollination which I would not have expected with such a lot of wind. But peas there were, and in such profusion that, on sunny days, the tundra was rich with their sweet, clovery smell.

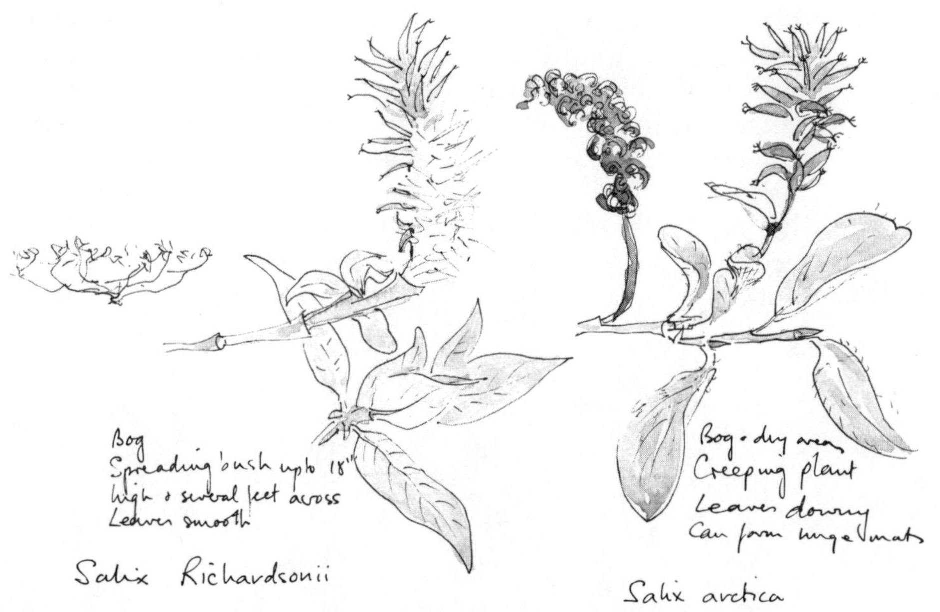

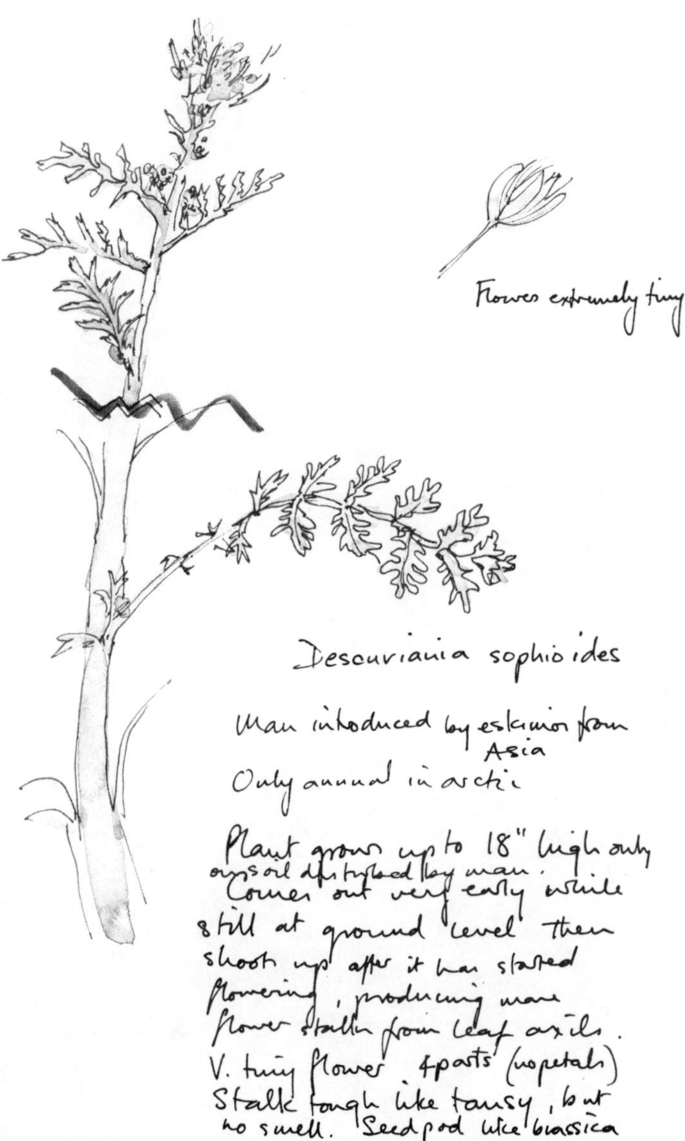

Everywhere among the tussocks were lemming burrows, and these fat, reddish, small-eyed rodents sat sometimes at the entrance to their holes, ready to whisk out of sight at the first hint of danger. Katie and Dennis' dog goes mad for them, rooting them up, then killing them, and burying them again. Their lime-white bones lie among the plants, such tiny, intricate skulls, such fragile, matchstick thighs. They were said to be at the top of their seven-year cycle — the predators, the foxes, weasels, and ookpiks, or snowy owls, would increase accordingly.

A pair of golden plovers laid four white, speckled eggs in a slight hollow of naked ground close to my tent. I would not have found the nest had the birds not demonstrated ceaselessly, running ahead and calling, or feigning broken wings as I walked past. The closer I got, the more agitated they became, until, when I was very near, one of the pair (the sexes are indistinguishable, but it was probably the female, for they have the strongest instinct to protect their young) flopped in pathetic panic right at my boots. The instant I drew away, the display lessened, and by gauging its intensity, I found the nest. The broken wing behaviour is supposed to draw away predators, but are the foxes not smart enough to learn that such activity means a meal? Or is their instinct geared only to the pursuit of an apparently helpless victim? Presumably the display works, or it would not have evolved. But I never found the eggs of ducks or geese, for they sit motionless among the grassy marshes and give no sign of their presence.

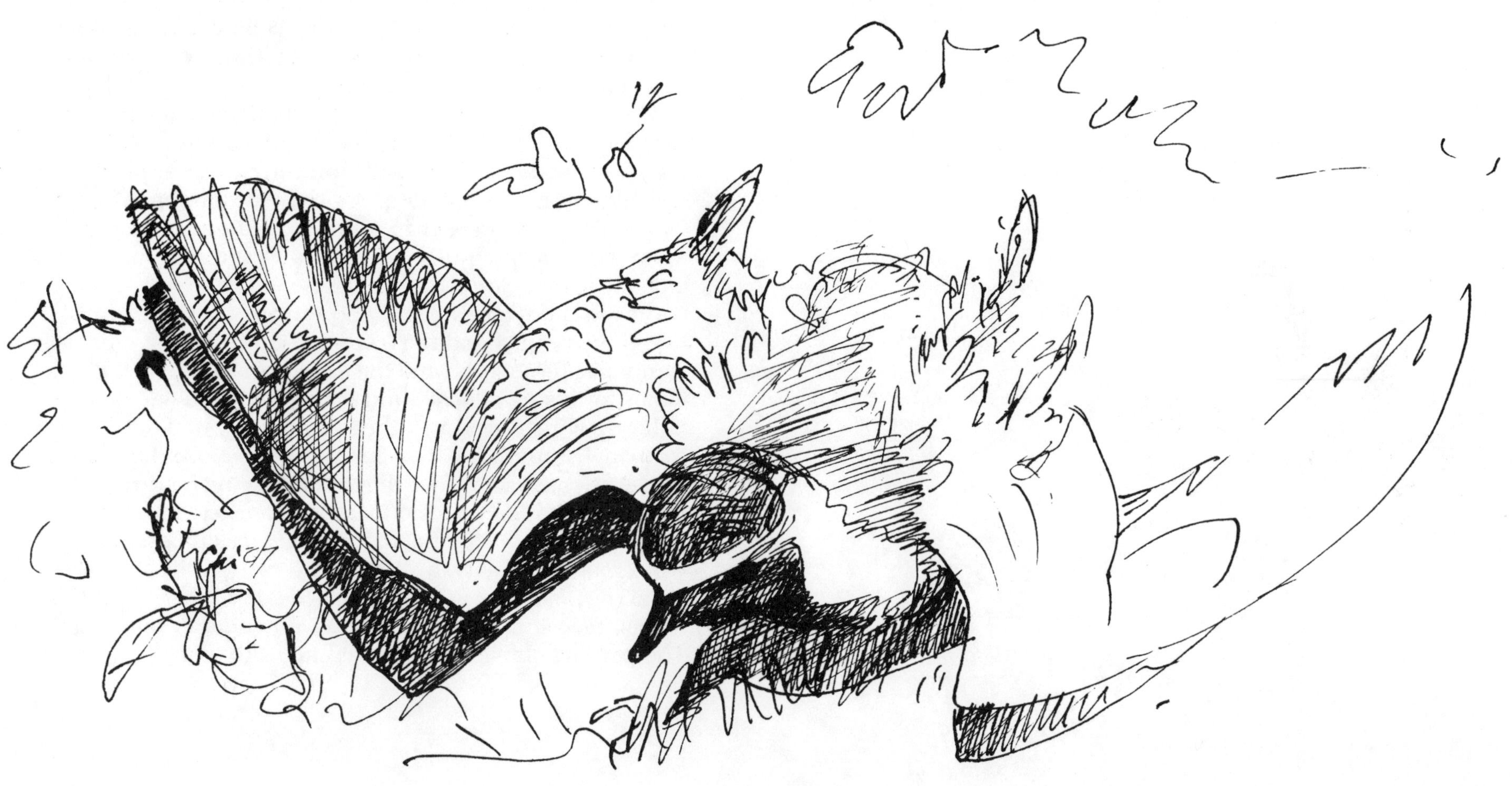

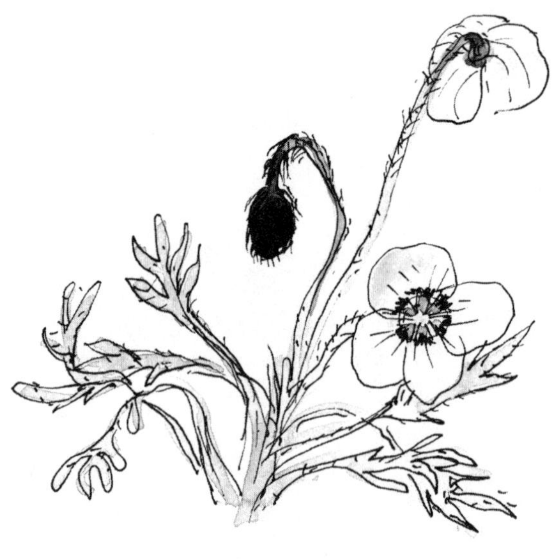

ARCTIC POPPY
Papaver radicatum

A mile from the camp is the sea. Not the wall to wall land-locked ice that constitutes the arm, but the open coast, beyond which, by many miles, is the mainland. One tends to forget that Canada has a northern coast, but Cambridge Bay is on an island, the third largest in the country. In spring, when the days were long, but the ice still good, some of The People went down to Yellowknife on snow machines. Yellowknife is at the northernmost tip of Canada's road system, 500 miles away.

There was, as always where the land ends, the mystery that the seashore has, a sense of magic and infinity of distance that the land, even the tundra, can never produce. For all that, it was a strange shore to walk upon. The sea was frozen and locked in stillness. No waves pounded upon the beach or pushed their scalloped scud and froth onto the stones. Small blue mussels clung to weed a foot or two from the water's edge, and on this narrow strip between the tundra and the ice, more flowers grew, thrifts, campions, lungworts, and the fragile arctic poppy with its lemon petals as delicate and crumpled as newly opened butterfly wings. And yet, these dainty poppy flowers are amazingly tough, for they thrust boldly above the tundra on slender stalks and face the sun, following it, drinking it, round and round on its everlasting journey.

It was never a silent shore, despite its stillness, for the wind roared ceaselessly and tugged my hair by the roots. An arctic loon, heavy-necked, beat against it with scythlike wings, then flung itself sideways, downwind, out to sea. The poppies danced and jerked and fluttered.

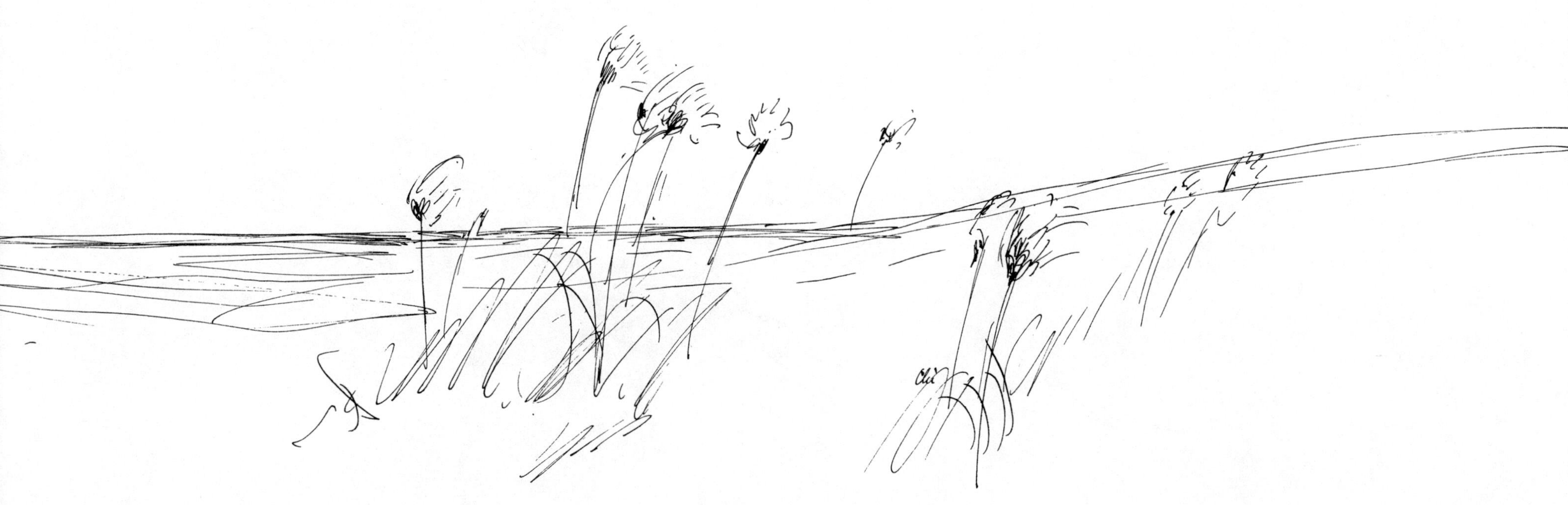

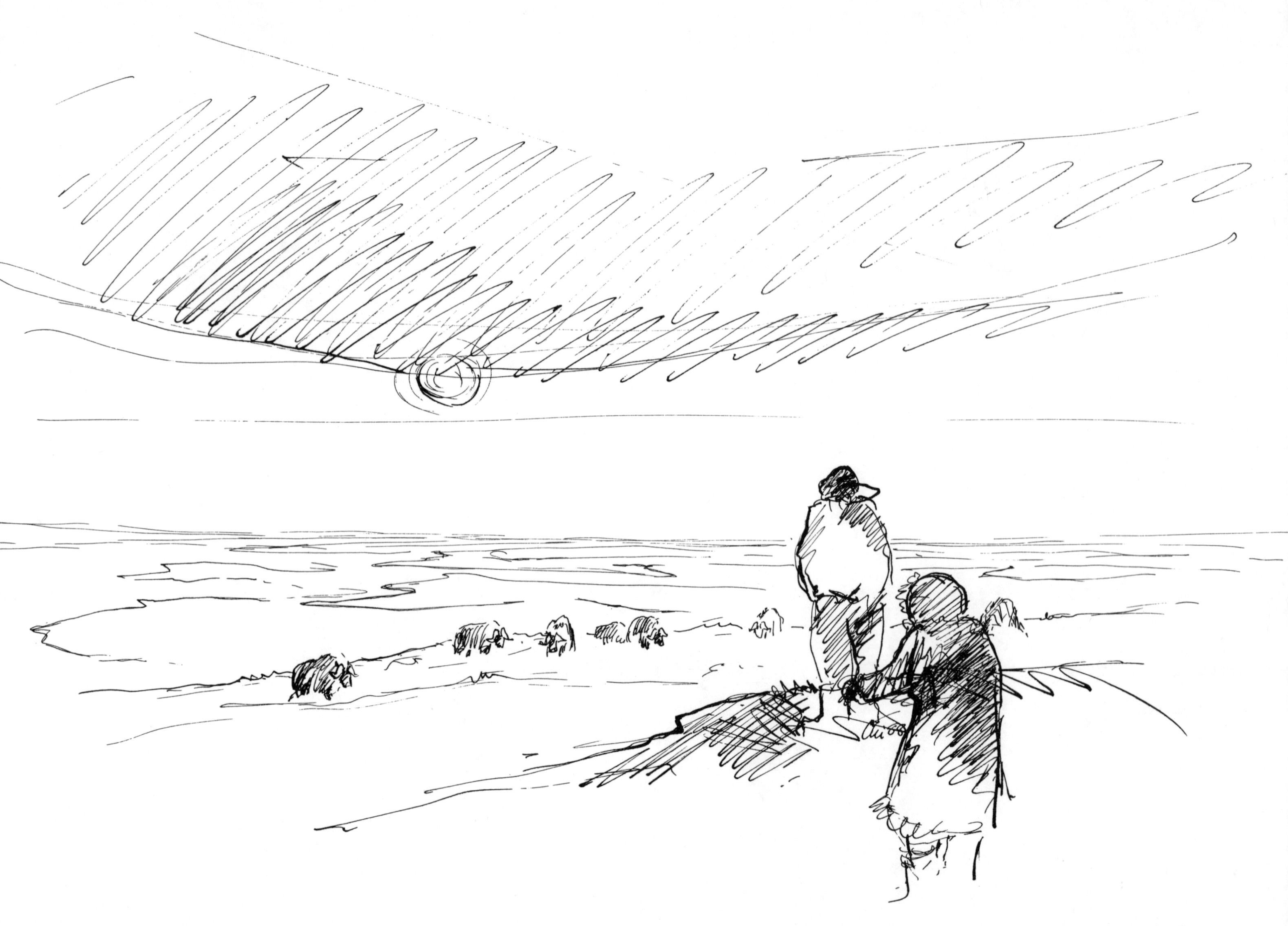

One day, I hiked for miles to a small peninsula of hills and frozen bays. A huge snowdrift clung to the lee of a slope, and from it, freshets ran, sparkling among the boulders down to the ice. It was a good place for lunch (though what the hours were, by the clock, I neither knew nor cared). My face ached from the wind and sun and glare. Everything was so pale: the rocks, the tundra, the sky, the sea. Even shadows were light and insubstantial. Far out to sea, two snowmobiles buzzed cautiously, looking for seals. I had seen these animals sometimes, black dots on the infinity of blinding ice, but heat waves made close objects dance like smoke and distant ones disappear or stand upside down. Through binoculars, the world writhed.

There was a sound of shots, then faint shouts, but the men were too far away for me to see if they had got anything.

Suddenly, there was a flicker of movement among the boulders. A lemming? No, a weasel. He was honey coloured with a neat white bib and a spindly black tail like a worn paintbrush. He was intensely curious, like all of his tribe. He looped nervously up to me, slim-bodied, carnivorous, ready to fly if I so much as batted an eye. He darted to my boot, and for one awful moment I thought he was going to run up my pants leg, for I felt his little paws on my ankle, and he shoved his nose and beady eyes into what must have seemed, to him, an interesting sort of lemming hole. I did not fancy having to dislodge him should he make the attempt. But he decided there was nothing up there for him, and he whisked around behind me and under my pack. I reached for my camera, but my movement disturbed him, and he was gone.

I was tired, and would have a long walk back to camp. At least I would not have to worry about being home before dark.

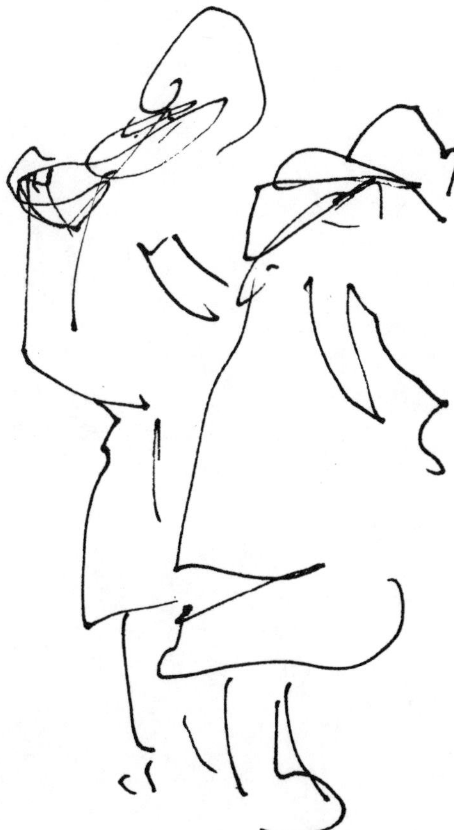

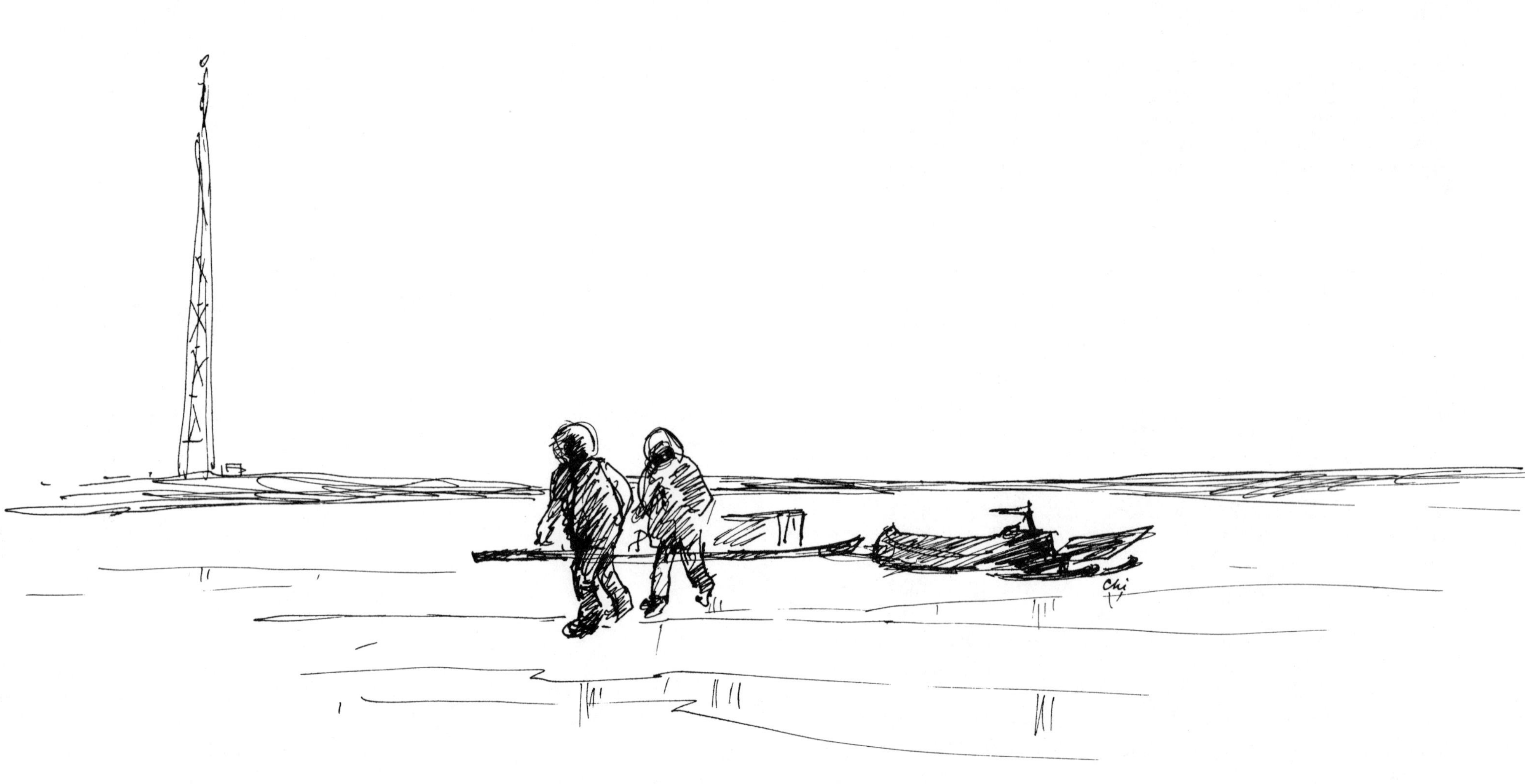

12th July

On Friday, July 10th, the mosquitos hatched. Small and feisty, they homed in on any part of my anatomy that was sheltered from the air movement. I sat facing the wind — my clothes would protect my back — but they bit my ankles through my woollen socks and nibbled at the backs of my ears. Still, I'd known worse. It is only further south, on the mainland, that these little bloodsuckers occur in such horrifying numbers.

This morning, a Sunday, is unbelievable. There is no wind. Everything is utterly still. I woke when the light was still golden and the shadows long, and the land sprawled motionless, tawny as a yellow-eyed cat. The shallow, amber-bottomed pond in the floor of the valley lay like a limpid jewel beneath the clear, cloudless, luminous sky. It was long before the townsfolk would be astir after the inevitable Saturday night partying, and there was no traffic, no human voice, only the thin, querulous whistle of the golden plover, the mew of the jaegers, the gossiping of the old squaw ducks, and the comfortable grunting of a pair of ptarmigan. What amazing eyebrows the ptarmigan has. Bright orange half moons that stick up like wings against his mottled, brown, summer plumage. He extends his neck and struts proudly, with fanned tail, the classic picture of a dominant male, while his drabber-coloured wife scuttles meekly behind.

In my wanderings along the coast, I have picked up broken pieces of plywood and two-by-fours, silvery with age, discarded by the cariboo hunters, and the sea. So I have a smouldering fire to keep the mosquitos at bay. Suddenly a shiver of blue speeds across the little pond, and the fire flutters into flames. The wind has begun.

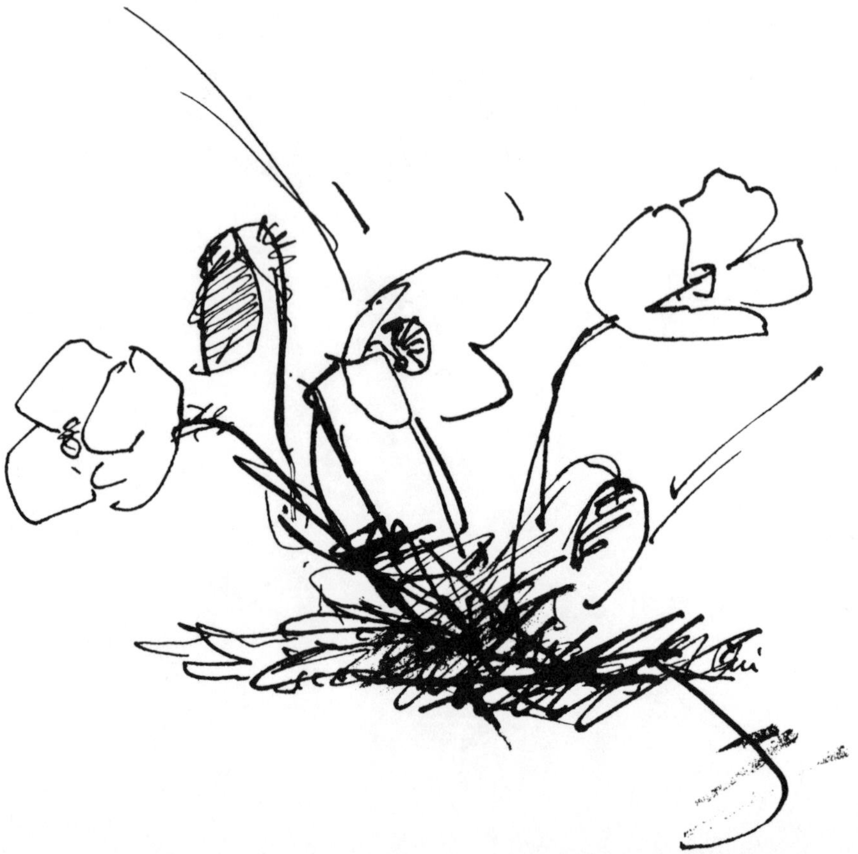

It is hot and airless inside the tent. There is no wind, and the mosquitos cling to the screen and patter like rain on the canvas, and their small shadows dance up and down the southern wall. It is very quiet. Even the birds lie still in these, the hottest hours of the day, and the only sound is the unvarying whine of the insects, in which individual performers are lost in a continuous, singing whole. I should be thankful that we have had enough summer to get them at all. Some years, it is just too cold.

I have moved camp to the other side of town, to the foot of Mt. Pelly. The country has changed considerably since my first trip out here three weeks ago. In town, a large wedge of open water has spread from the mouth of the river into the sea in front of the Hudson's Bay Company store, and it is hard to believe that, six days before, people were walking out there and driving snowmachines. The pinpricks of flowers that had begun to open among the dogs and garbage along the waterfront have erupted into tangled thickets of blooms up to six or eight inches high. Some of the petals have faded and dropped, and already seeds are forming.

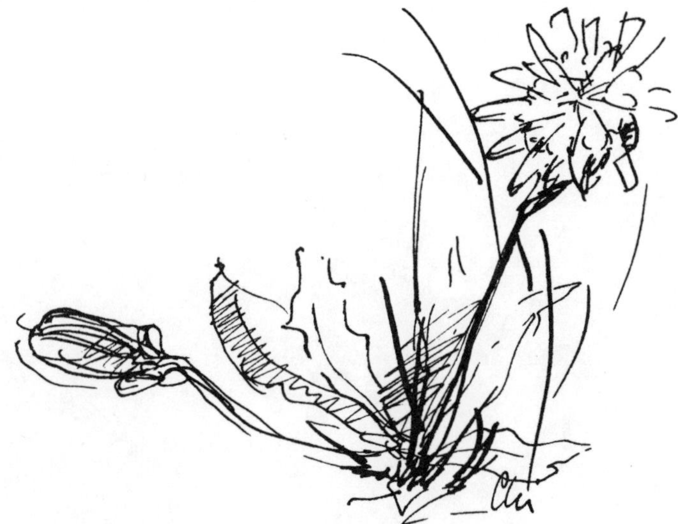

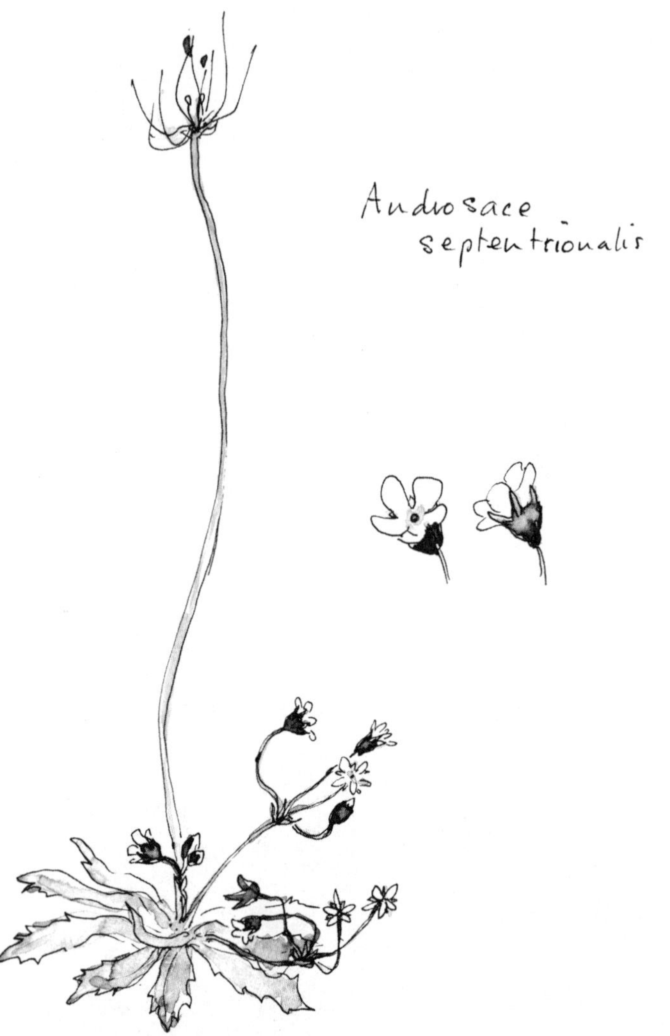

Out here, the tundra is greening, and the stony ridges are massed with flowers, purple oxytropes, creamy avens, pink wallflowers, and armies of yellow poppies, nodding in the wind. Most of the ice has gone from the freshwater ponds, and people are fishing from power boats, buzzing round in tight circles in the lower, deeper parts of the river.

The Inuit have followed the fish and moved from this area, and I am almost alone. My tent is perched on a ridge to catch the breeze, and in this treeless country I can see forever. Nearby is a coffin-shaped hole walled shallowly with rocks. It has been there a long time, for orange scabs of lichen have blurred the outlines, and mats of a spiky-leafed saxifrage smother the lower layers. It is easy to imagine a small, skin-clad man, lying there in wait for cariboo. I fit my body into the hole; it is too cramped for me. The mountain swells behind like a breaking wave, as it did when the skin-clad man lay there, but now, to the west, the uncompromising roofs of town and domes of the DEW line station shine, tiny, but perfectly clear, some dozen miles away. And still the tundra rolls beyond. The land is laced with holes like a paper doily, each filled with water and a mirror to the sky. Further still, almost at the edge of discernible vision, and insubstantial with the heat waves which dance upon it, is the thin, white line of the ice on the open sea.

There is a clink and clatter of stones as I walk. I'm told that these rocks, which lie like heaps of broken pottery, are a very old limestone. This means they were formed beneath the sea. The mountain itself was underwater 10,000 years ago, but that is not long by geological standards. White shells still lie about the summit, and as the sea subsided, it left raised beaches, giant steps of gravel, particularly at the north end. Probably, the land is still rising.

But the rocks were ancient long before their last drowning. A man in town has done some diving by the wreck of Amundsen's "Maude," which juts the remnants of its wooden ribs above the water near the old stone church in the bay. He says sea anemones and starfish, and all manner of soft-bodied creatures thrive beneath the surface. I would not have thought such animals would have survived the long winter dark. Do the organisms that form limestone live in these waters? Or was it warmer once? Or have these rocks travelled from other latitudes, carried by the inexorable movements of the earth?

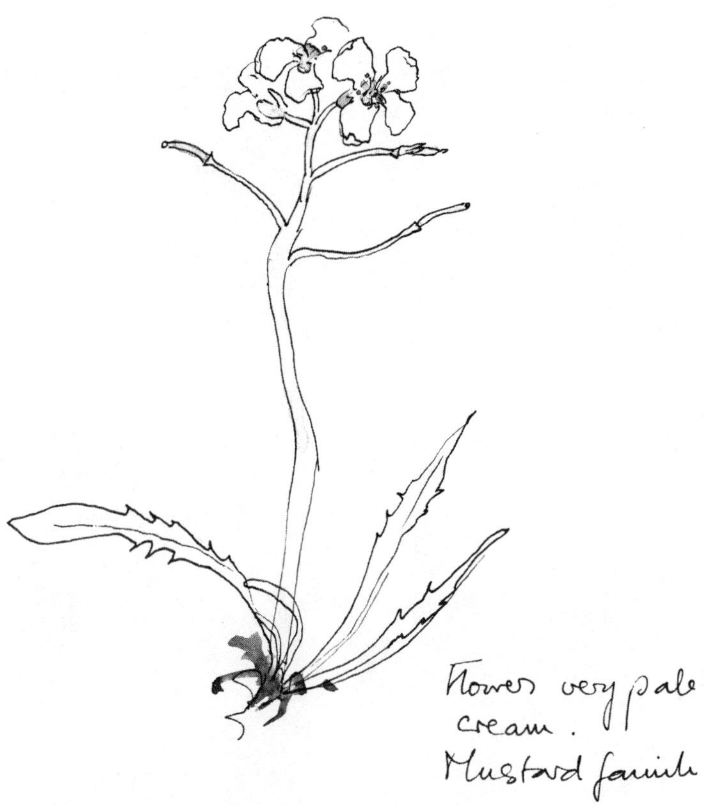

This is Oomingmak country. Their soft down lies snagged on the lichens and willow bushes, and their droppings and cowlike tracks are everywhere on the tundra. Once I saw a herd with calves, at a great distance, and assumed they were the same animals we had seen on my first trip out here, but mostly I find bulls in groups of two or three, grazing among the knee-high willows in the swamps. They are hard to approach, for there is little cover, and their eyes and sense of smell are sharp. One morning, there were three of them a mile or so below camp. Close by was a gently sloping gravel ridge, maybe three or four feet high, which did not look very promising, as cover. But the wind was right, and by bending double and scuttling through the swamp like a wounded plover, I made the ridge undetected, finishing the distance on elbows and stomach.

The three bulls were about 100 yards away, lying down and dozing like lumpy, misshapen hearth rugs. Others had stalked the Oomingmak in this place, for close by was an eyeless, whitened skull with enormous grinding teeth and a great, bony hornboss.

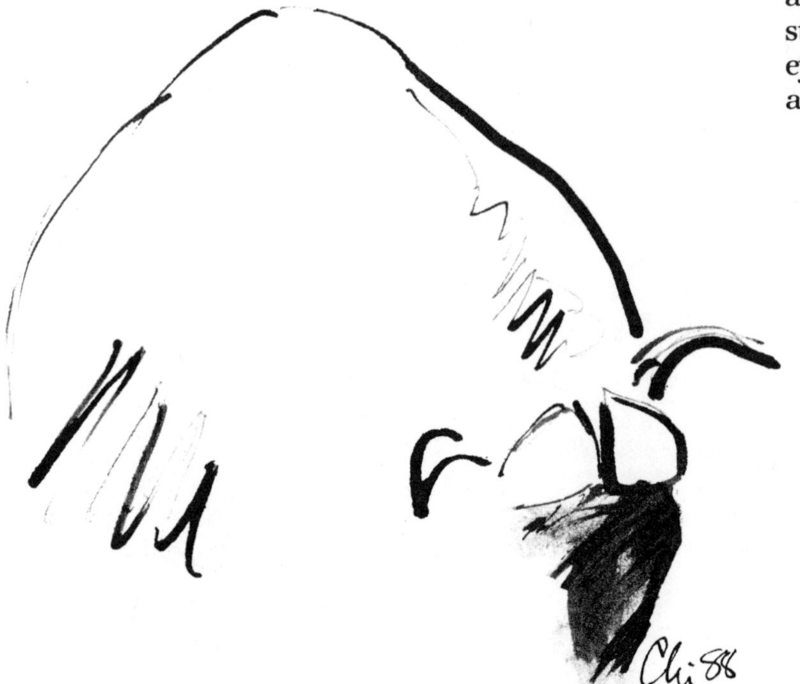

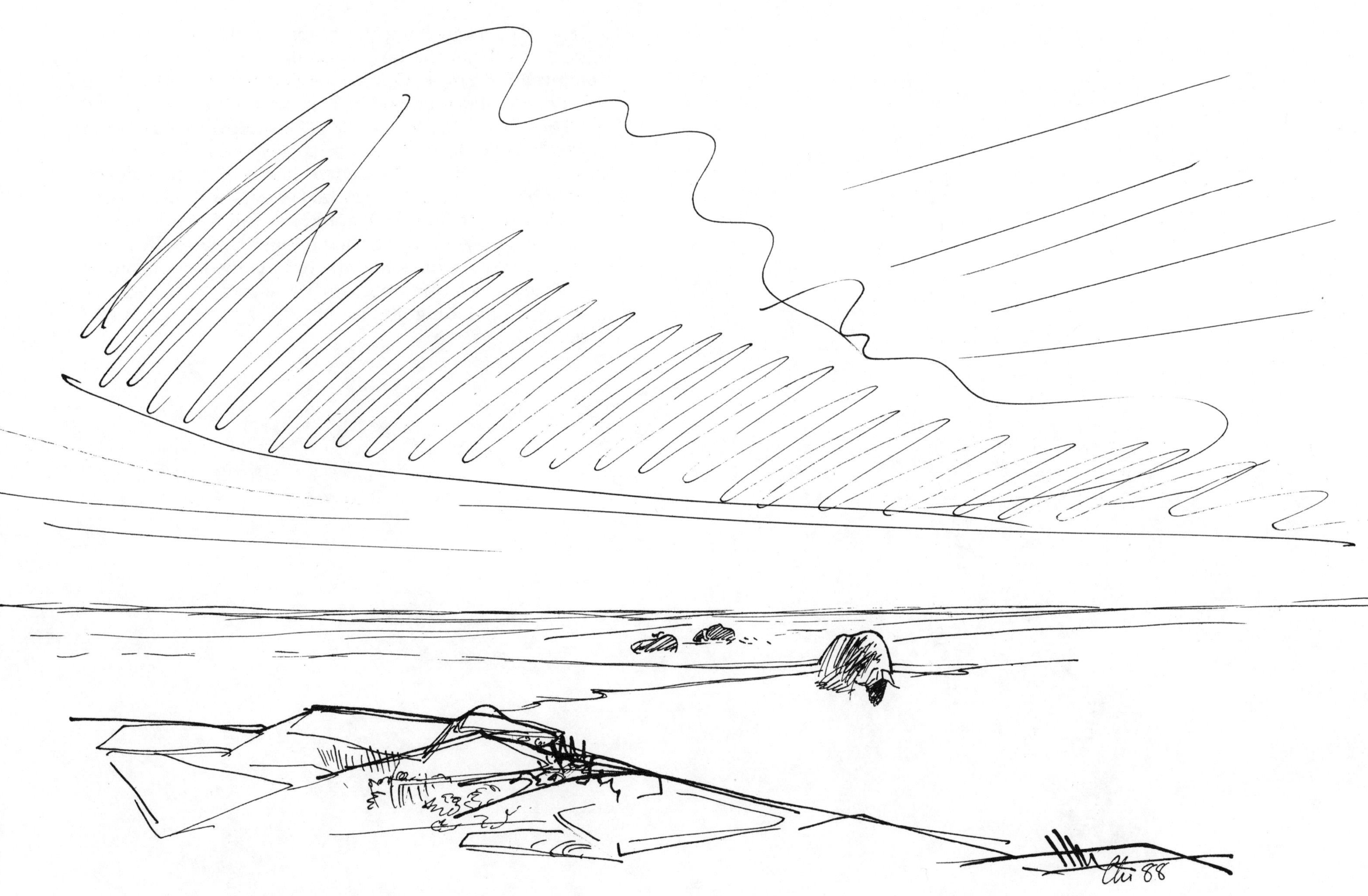

It was pleasant lying there, for the breeze was fresh enough to dispel the bugs, and the sun was warm and comfortable on my back. For awhile, the bulls did nothing except chew their cud and flick an occasional ear against a fly. Then there was a movement. I focussed the camera in excited anticipation. Bull #1 began to rise. He straightened his front legs, sitting for awhile like a dog, then slowly hauled his hindquarters upright. His back was toward me, and through the lens, all I could see was a hairy mound with a few tangled rags of down hanging from the sides. Hardly photographic material, and I waited, eye screwed to the viewfinder and finger hovering over the trigger, for him to do something interesting. He lay down again and went back to sleep.

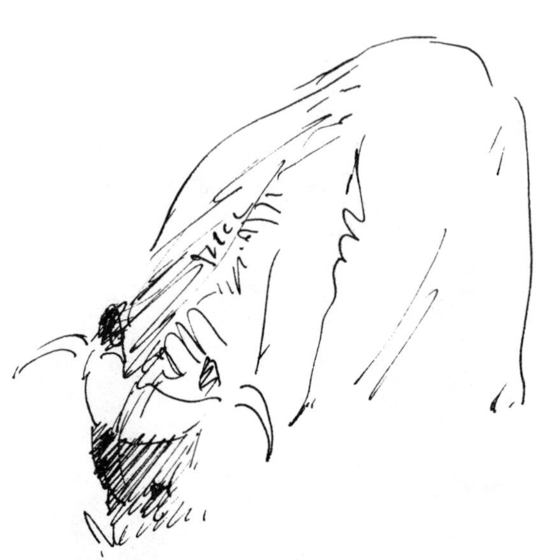

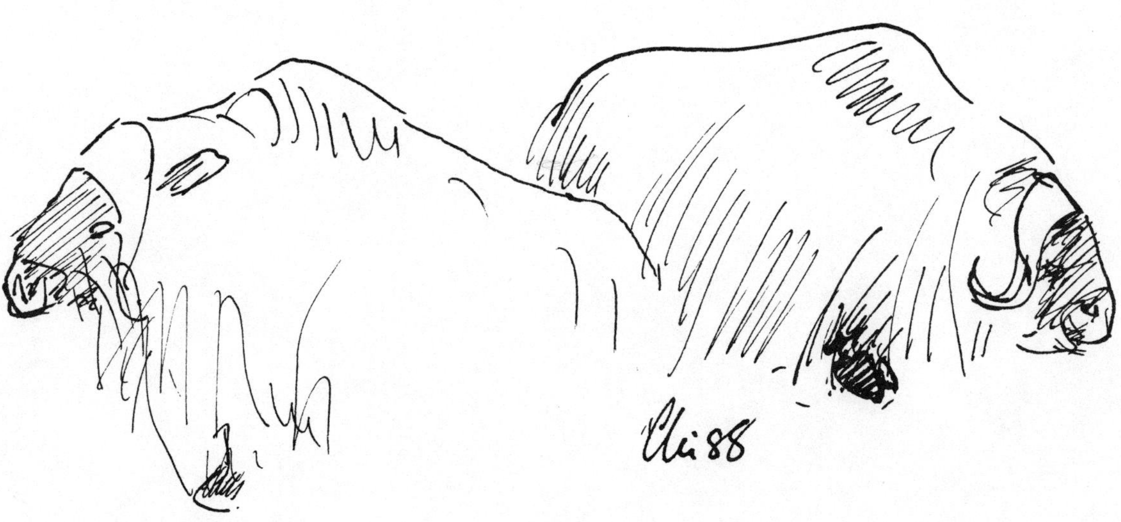

Black-capped terns fluttered slow white wings as they hovered over the nearest lake hunting small fish. A sandpiper flew to a rock six feet from my head and preened himself. My elbows began to ache, and a small stone pressed uncomfortably against my breastbone. I shifted slightly, and the sandpiper flew away. Bull #2 got up, turned round, and lay down again. A big orange bumblebee flew by. A pair of crane flies, glued end to end in a mating embrace, waved twelve long legs uselessly as each tried to take the other in tow. Bull #3 heaved himself to his feet. He paused. He took a few steps and began to feed. This was better. Slowly he ate a path through the willow bushes and started on the short grass in the swamp in front of me.

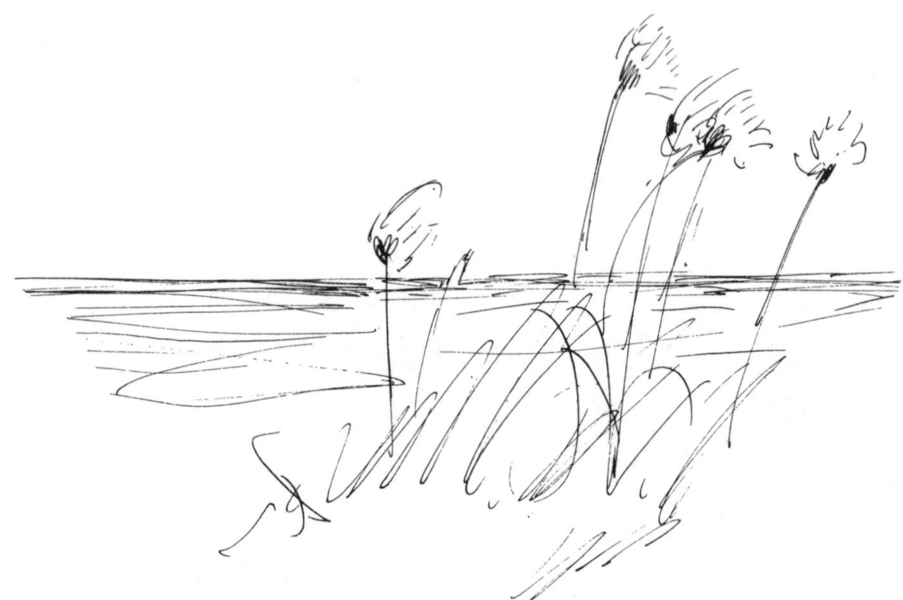

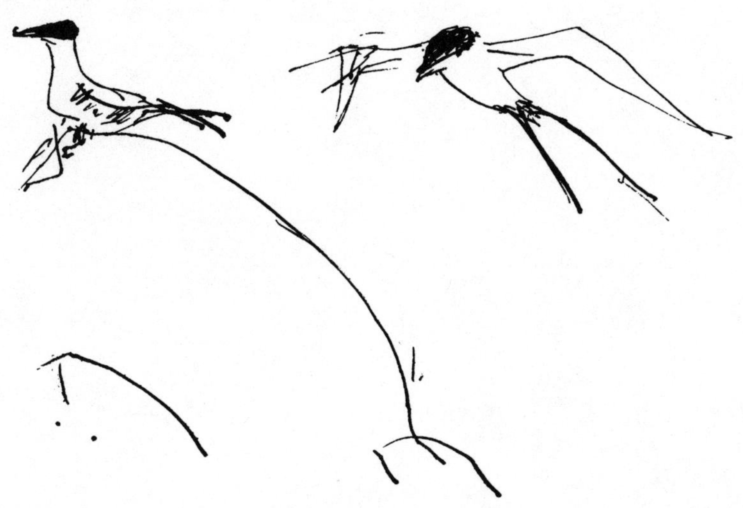

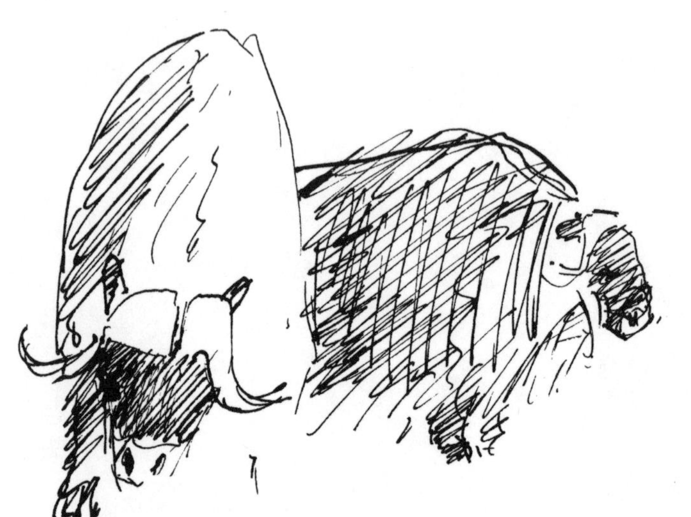
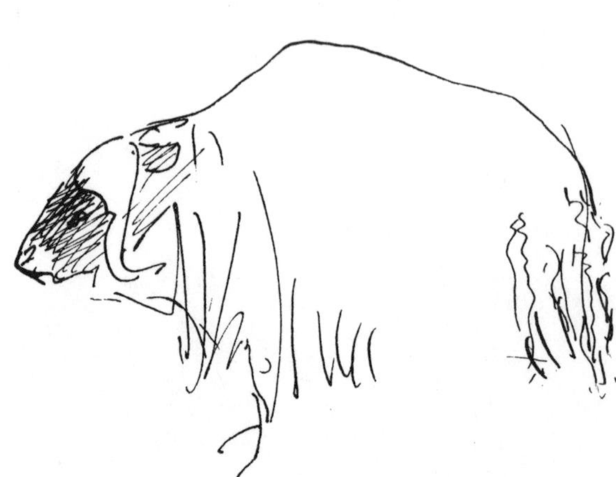

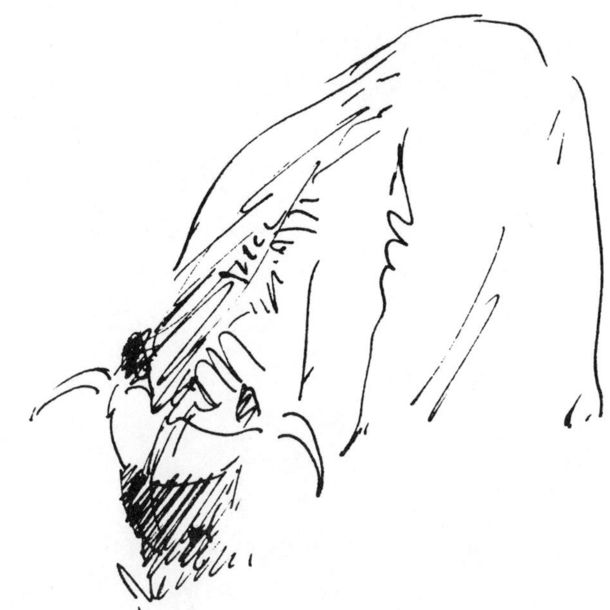

The camera clicked surreptitiously, then again and again as he gradually reduced the distance between us. I could hear the tearing sound as he ripped up mouthfuls of grass. I did not have a very powerful lens, but through the viewfinder I could distinguish the long, silky hairs of his eyelashes. How close was it wise for me to be? Bulls were known to be belligerent, although they usually stopped before their charge was consummated, but if he did come, there was absolutely nowhere for me to hide. I had once seen one run from a trike, and gallop through the hummocky, waterlogged swamp as if it were the best racing turf, then straight up the steep side of Mt. Pelly. The trike, on the road, hadn't a hope in catching him. The bull's massive head and shoulders were designed to batter against a thousand-pound rival, and I would have little chance if he decided to come at me.

But encounters with wildlife that end in injury for the human animal are rare. The bull turned slowly and gazed back toward his friends. I elbowed my way backwards down the ridge and scuttled, crabwise, through the swamp. My pictures would not rock the naturalist world, but they would be good enough for me.

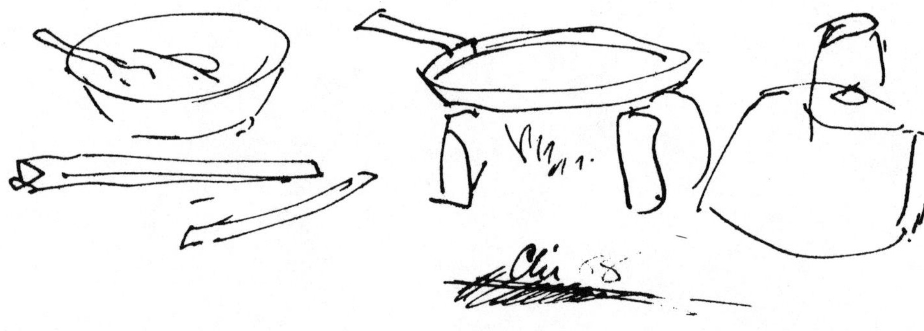

Friday started fresh and clear, but the afternoon grew oppressive and buggy, and a grey haze diffused the sky. The sun simply dissappeared, dissolved, like a lozenge. A black wall of cloud marched in from the north, swallowing the land.

The storm started as a warm, gentle rain, and I battened down the tent and sweated in the breathless gloom. Then the wind struck. The canvas flapped and boomed, and the external framework of poles hummed like harp strings. My little nest felt vulnerable perched upon the ridge, but it survived a fitful night, and later, when the worst of the rain had stopped, I decided to move camp. There was a quarter of an inch of water in containers left out of doors (I'd had the presence of mind to weight all pots and cups and plates with stones), and the wind blew strong and cold and gusty from the north. There was no sign of a mosquito.

In the lee of the ridge, the wind still swirled and eddied, but it was not so violent. Tent pegs were ineffectual in this country, and the only thing that held the canvas down were rocks which lined the bottoms of the walls inside. The Inuit had anchored their skin shelters this way, and their ovals of lichen-encrusted stones could still be found.

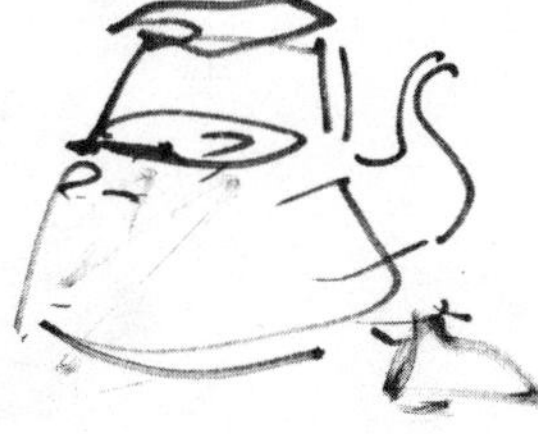

I should have collapsed the tent before removing the boulders, but I thought it would be easier to haul them out with the walls still standing. Too late, I realized my mistake, and, as I crawled backwards through the doorway, clutching the last boulder to my breast, the fabric leapt into the air like a kite, and one of the aluminum poles crumpled. When I tried to straighten it, it snapped.

So there I was, without shelter, in threatening rain, twelve miles from town, with gear too heavy to pack unaided. The tent was an old one, and it alone must have weighed sixty pounds.

I lugged the deflated canvas and tangle of poles to safer ground, immediately throwing rocks on it to keep it there. As before, I had salvaged firewood from the abandoned campsites along the lake. I had carried home three backpack loads among which was a longer piece of two-by-two, and with this and a spare bit of rope I splinted the pole. The canvas walls rose again, and it seemed the repair would hold. The wind lessened, and fingers of fog crept around the mountain and blanketed the world in a clammy shroud. I lay in my new berth in my sleeping bag, perfectly comfortable.

But on the Sunday, I hitched a ride back to town with a family of Inuit in the back of a pickup truck. It was as well I did, for the storm renewed itself with double fury. Katie and Dennis were not so lucky. They had bought a new canvas tent (their nylon, backpacking one had disintegrated first time out) with specially reinforced steel poles, and had set it upon the ridge close to where mine had been. All Sunday night they moved around to try and keep out of the drips. The heavy steel poles became permanently bent. At 4 A.M., they gave up and packed to come home. They passed many collapsed Inuit tents on the way in.

Today the weather is just as bad. I would not have thought I would have been so glad to be in the house.

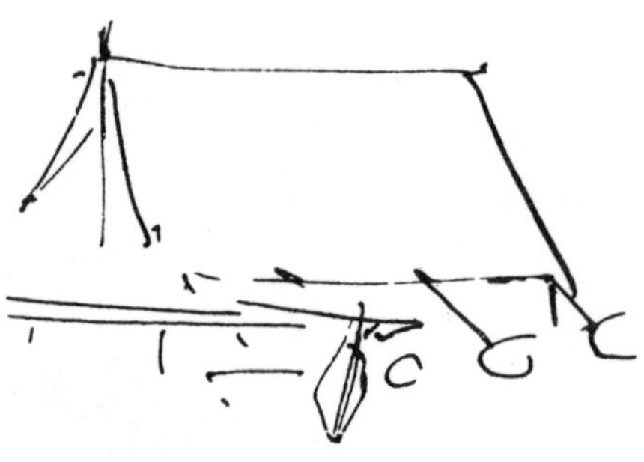

22nd July

Susan Mackay, whose house I am occupying, remains something of an enigma. Katie tells me the little blond boy in the photograph is adopted. She already has two grown children. Their rather dark, narrow-featured faces stare complacently from a pair of large studio portraits above a pink, frilly valentine's heart and a card with purple irises inscribed, across the front, in curly letters of gold, "From a Loving Husband." Katie has never seen the husband and doesn't know where he is.

Imagine my shock when he walks in one day. Especially as Susan Mackay's once immaculate front room is littered with painting materials and bits of plants and unfinished works. I started drawing the flowers in an attempt to capture their diversity, for reference books were hopelessly inadequate, and my first films have come back overexposed. The strong, washed-out light had fooled the metre, a common problem for beginner photographers out here. Now the flowers have become an obsession with me, and I have collected fifty species; samples of many of them sit in jars and cups and bowls, and drying papers lie so thickly on the floor, it is difficult to walk about. Thank goodness Katie's mother, who is visiting for two weeks and sharing the house with me, had done the pile of dishes in the sink.

"I promise I will clean it up before Susan comes back," I say, ashamed, waving helplessly at the mess.

But Jim Mackay had not noticed. He is swarthy, could be Spanish, but comes from British Columbia. The grown children take after him. "I just called round to see if you had any problems," he said. "I no longer live with my wife, but we still have a good relationship. I told her I'd keep an eye on the house.

"Everything seems to be fine. The sewage backed up into the bathtub one day, but they must not have realized anyone was living here, because when I got them to pump the tank, everything was O.K." Jim Mackay evinces no surprise at this; it is a common occurrence. Sewage and water are both stored in tanks in the houses and pumped into or out of trucks. In summer, water is hauled directly from a tundra pond, and in winter, blocks of ice are carted to a heated reservoir and melted. Trucking is cheaper than maintaining pipelines in this climate. Sewage is hauled out of town and dumped. It cannot drain through the permafrost, so eventually percolates through a green, luscious swamp into the sea. The sewage and water trucks look identical, but they haven't got them mixed up yet.

"I really appreciate being able to use the place. Especially in this kind of weather." I indicate the window, where the storm rages.

"That's O.K. It's good to have someone living in the place with so much vandalism about. Help yourself to meat. I keep my wife well supplied." He goes to the freezer and flings up the lid. It is full of cariboo lumps, unwrapped, with bits of hair and tundra frozen to them.

"Thanks," I say, "I will." But I don't eat cariboo meat much. It is amazingly tender and has a good taste, but its smell, when roasting, is nauseating. I prefer muskox, which I buy from the Hunters and Trappers association at a much cheaper rate than beef flown up from the south. It tastes like beef, but better, although it has a rather stringy texture and is better eaten ground.

27th July

Press your fingers hard into the groove behind your ear. It hurts. Imagine a piece of string looped from your ear to that of an opponent who is sitting on the floor opposite you and pulling backwards. And, if you can tolerate the pain, imagine it happening again and again until you defeat all contenders and the back of your ear is sore and bleeding.

Or lie on your stomach and raise your body rigid as if you were doing pushups, but instead of flattening the palms of your hands against the floor, clench your fists and balance on your knuckles. Then bounce around the room, touching the ground only with your knuckles and toes. You would need bandaids after that one too.

Or hang a small, model seal from a string higher than you can reach, and leap up and kick it and land on the same foot with which you kicked, without falling over. If you could do these things, or fillet a fish, or cook bannock over an open fire, or skin a seal, you would have been eligible for the eighteenth annual Northern Games, which were held in Cambridge Bay last weekend.

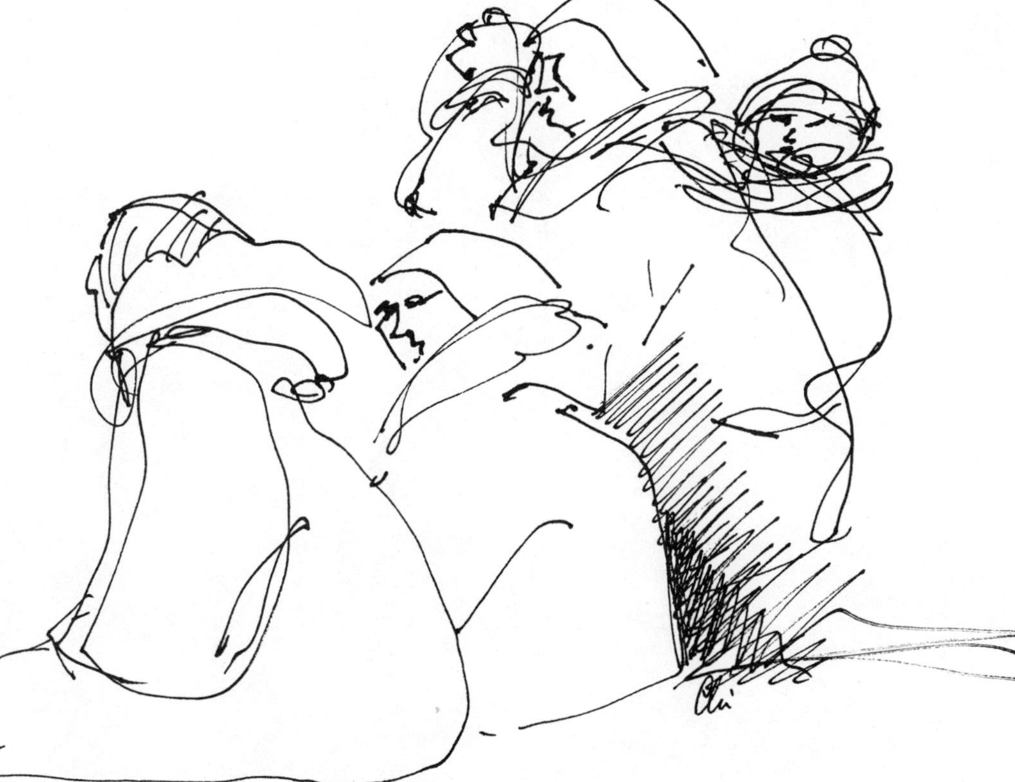

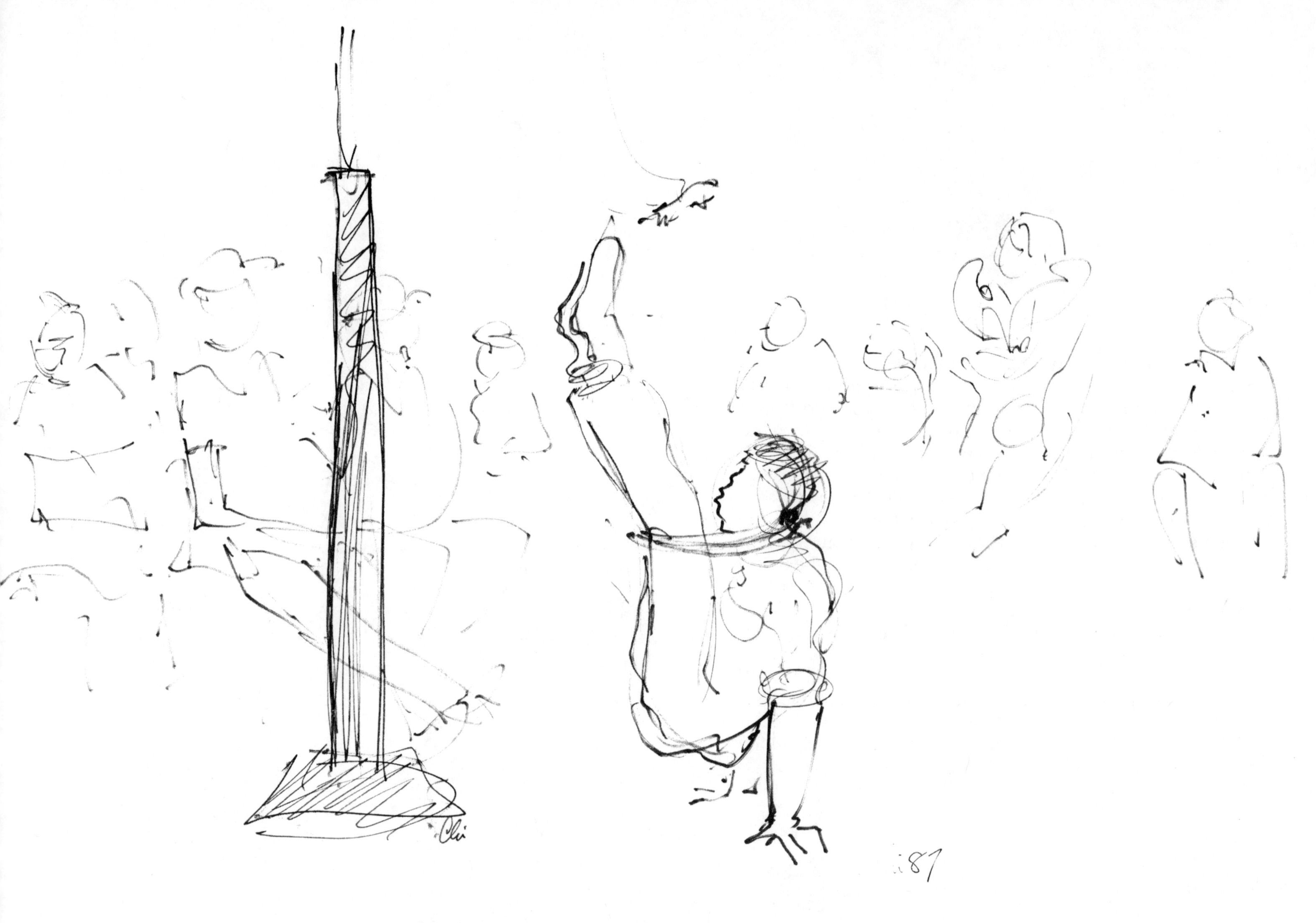

Teams came from all over the northern Arctic, from Inuvik, Gjoa Haven, Pelly Bay, Coppermine, and Bay Chaimo, and they were composed of a variety of people, for although the one-foot-high kick and the knuckle hop required the strength, agility, balance and youth of a ballet dancer, other events tested the skills of the traditional way of life, and it was the older people, and the women, who had these.

One thing was obvious throughout. Sportsmanship, in the true sense of the word, was very important. The winner was applauded, but not as much as the loser who tried his best, and the games were fought with an intensity I had good reason to remember, for, at 2 A.M. on Saturday morning, my name was called for the ladies' muskox fight.

I shook hands with my opponent, and we dropped to our hands and knees, and tucked our heads under each other's shoulders, and pushed. Our toes scrabbled for purchase on the smooth floor of the school gym. My opponent was far shorter than I, but twice as broad, and we grunted and strained, it seemed, forever. Her breath panted in my ear, and her long, clean-smelling hair half suffocated me. At first, I felt myself slide to the edge of the marked circle, but suddenly the other woman wilted, and I had won. I was so dizzy, I don't know how I found my way to my seat. All too soon, it was time to fight another bout. I lost that one; I could not match my opponent's sheer desire to win.

The bannock making and tea boiling races, the fish cutting and the harpoon throwing were held outside in the playground. Our fingers grew greasy from bannock and fried fish, and the smell of muskox burgers wafted over from the concession stand. On Sunday, a cold wind blew, and it started to rain. After the seal skinning, we moved indoors, and the duck plucking made surprisingly little mess, for the eider feathers were rain-damp and the women's nimble fingers allowed only a few pieces of snow-soft down to escape the plastic bags. As we were sitting there, it was decided to proceed with events previously

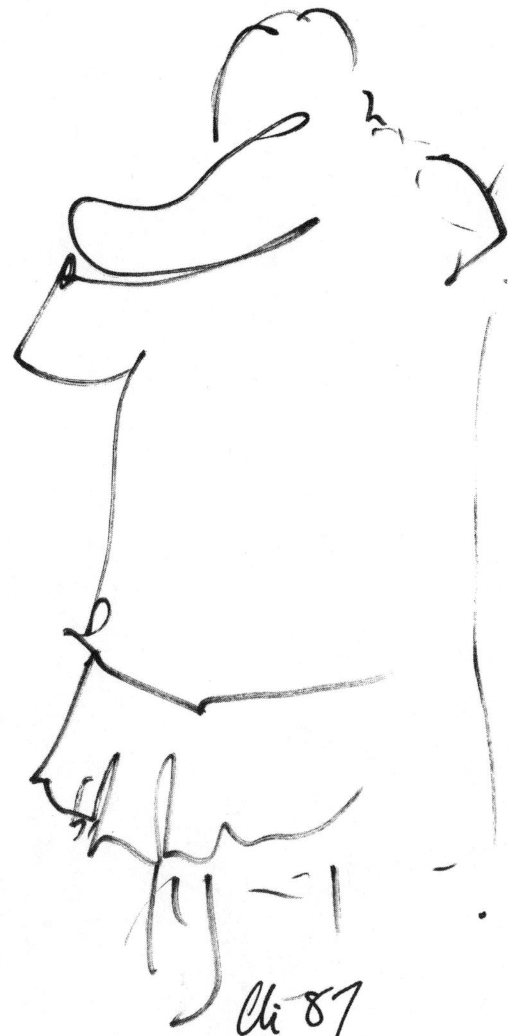

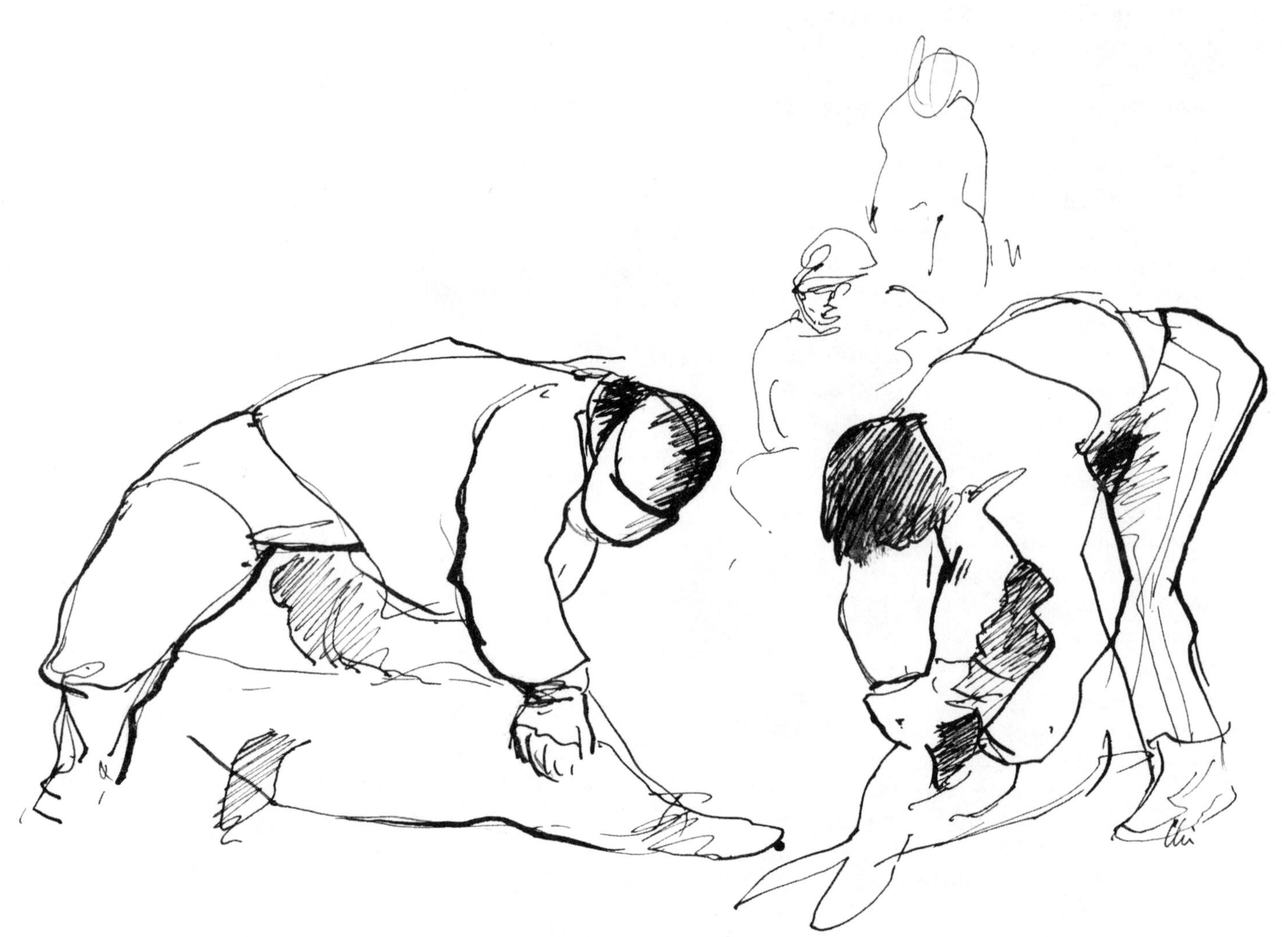

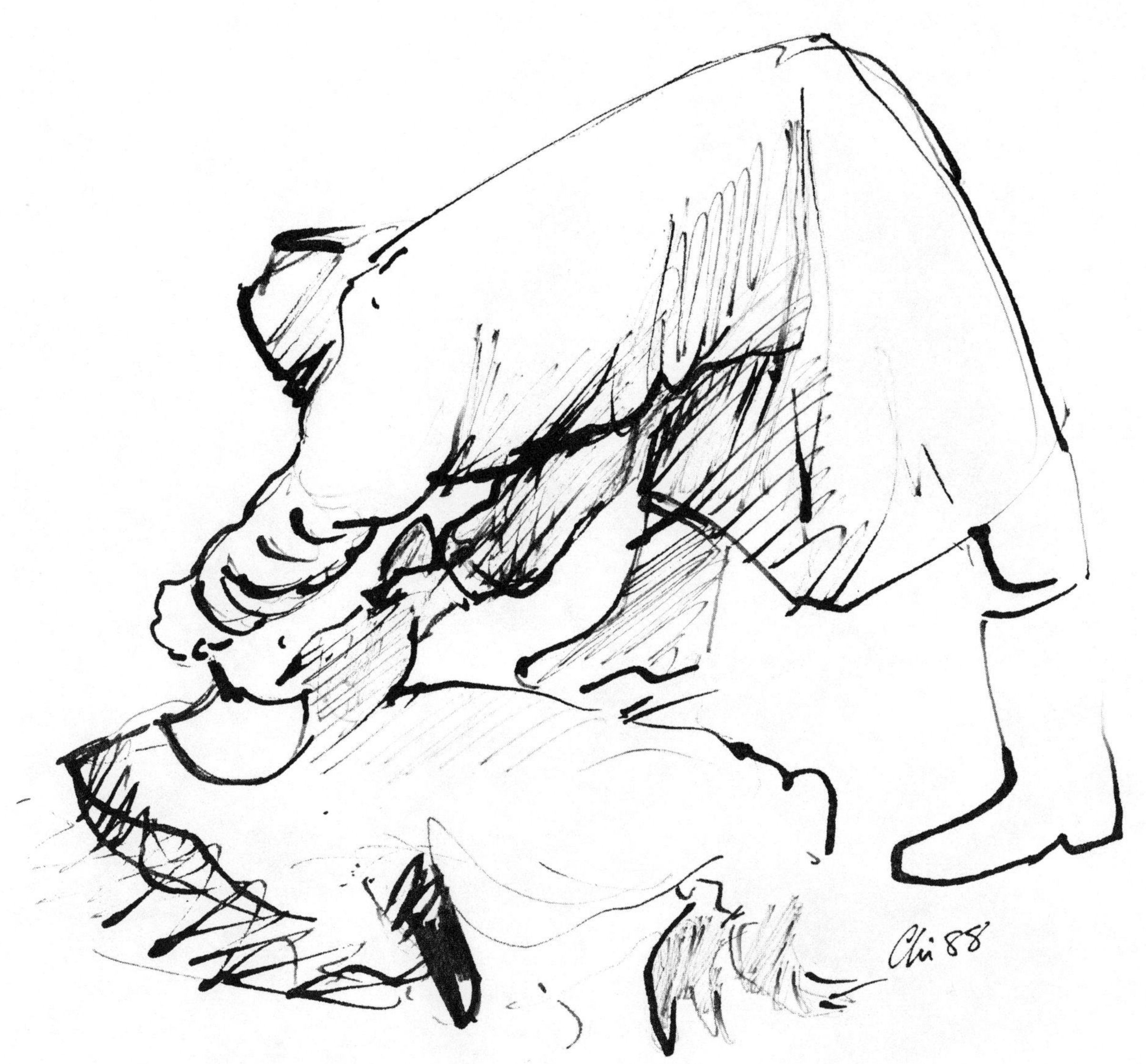

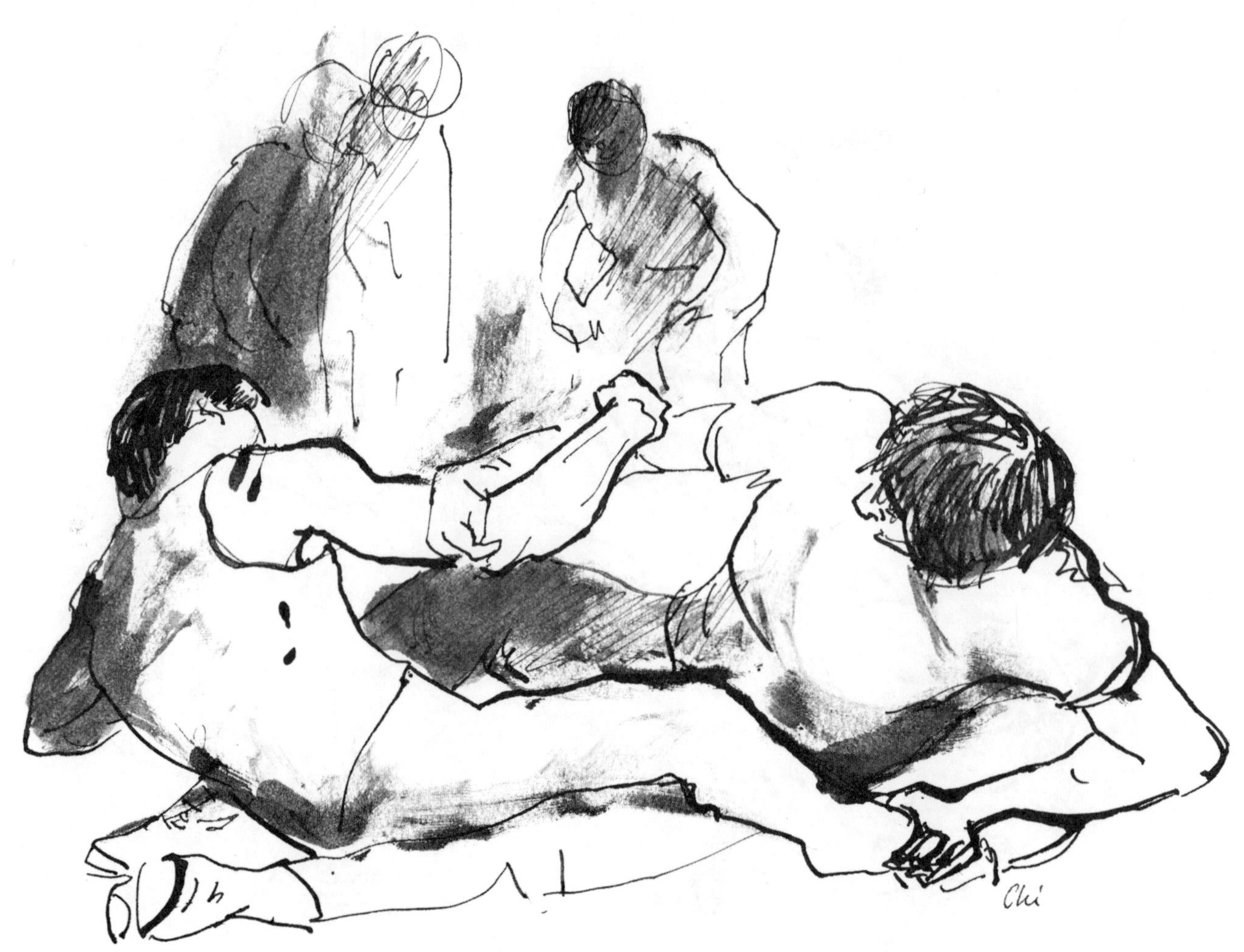

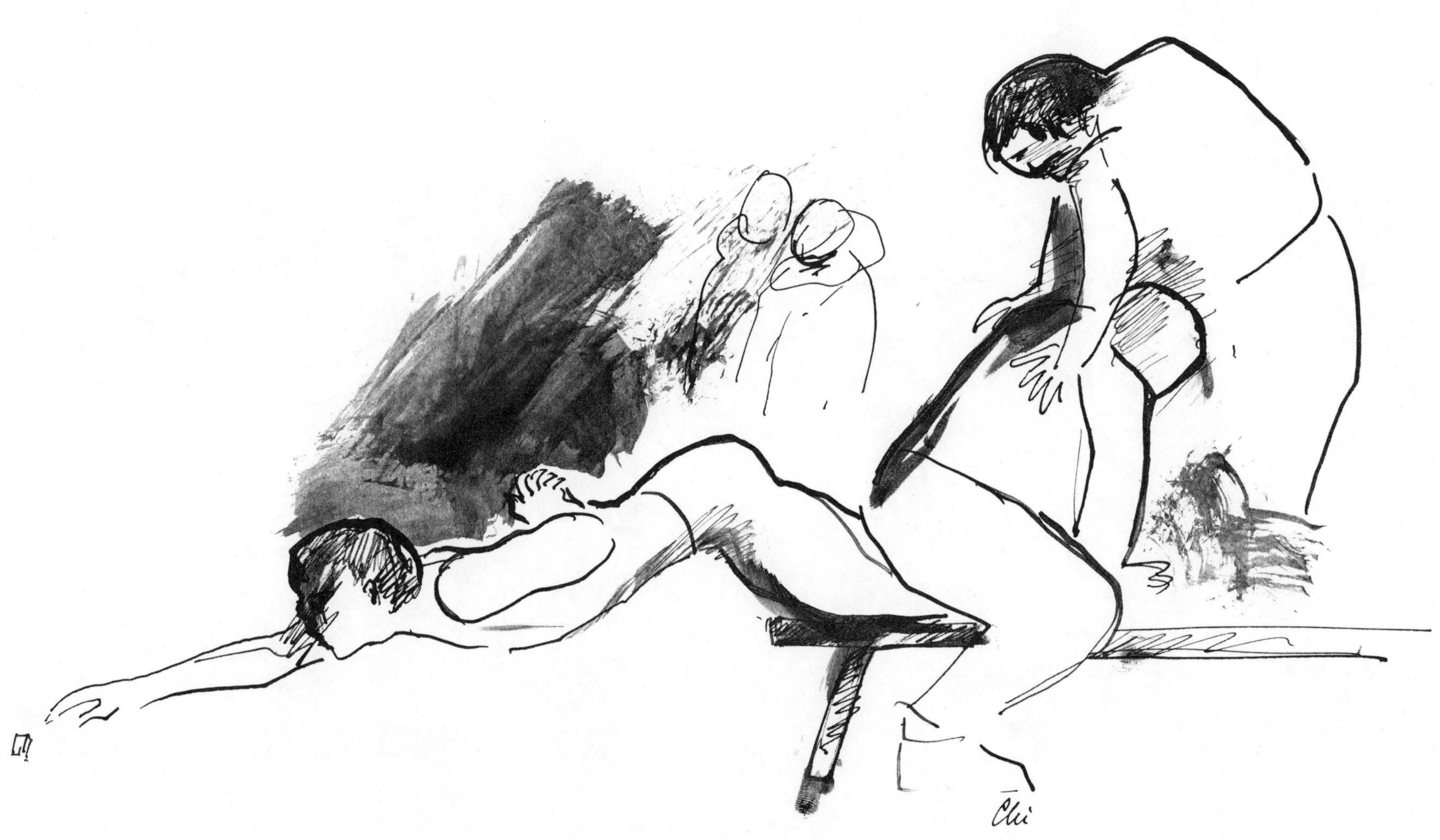

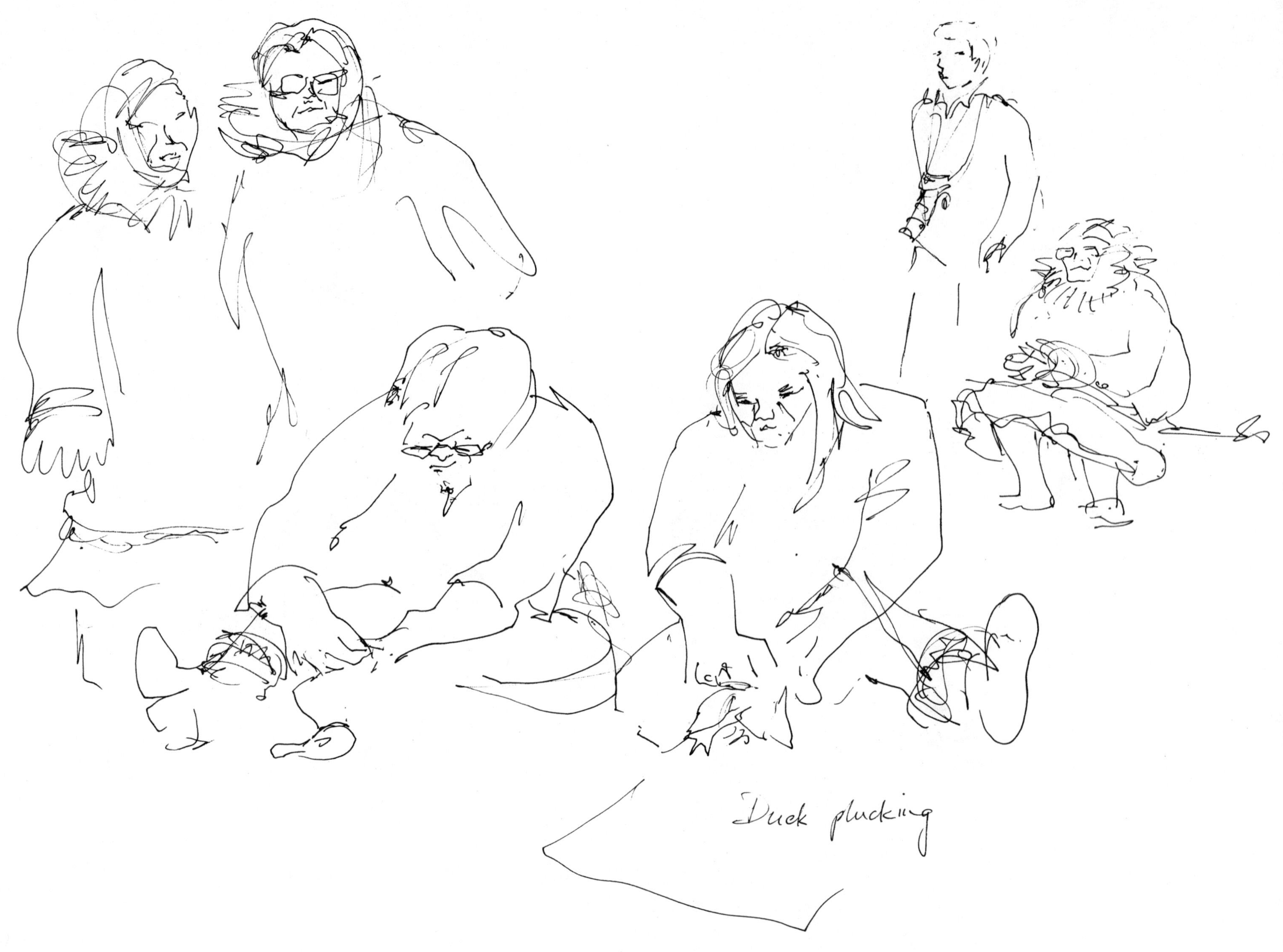

Duck plucking

designated for the evening, and after a while, a supper
break was announced. "And when we all return," said the
man with the megaphone, "we will have the ladies' arm
pull." What a wonderful way to run a schedule.

The bench reach was one of the more spectacular com-
petitions. The contestant knelt on the end of a bench, facing
outwards. Two heavyweights sat on his feet to anchor him,
while two more sat on the other end of the bench to hold it
down. The contestant had to lean forward until his body
was horizontal, and place a matchbox beyond the reach of
his fellows. Then (and this is where the cords in his neck
became rigid and his face turned purple with effort), he
had to return to his original position without touching the
ground. Everyone eventually fell flat on his face.

There was a jigging contest, jig as in dance as opposed to
fish — which lonely Irishman had introduced that? — and
a drum dance, where the chanting and booming of the
skin-covered hoop, and the swinging of the fringed and
intricately patterned fur clothing made it easy to forget the
bland neon light and flashing cameras, and see instead the
encircling walls of the igloo leaping with the shadows of
the seal oil lamp. And finally, there was the medal pre-
sentation followed by the square dance, but I gave them a
miss: I had to sleep sometime.

A new day was beginning as I walked out into the
rain-sweet night. The sun, teetering on the rim of the
world, lay in a slit of molten gold under the heavy roof of
overcast, and threw a dim and bloody light over the town.
And there was a rainbow, a huge red, midnight rainbow,
arching through the zenith of the sky.

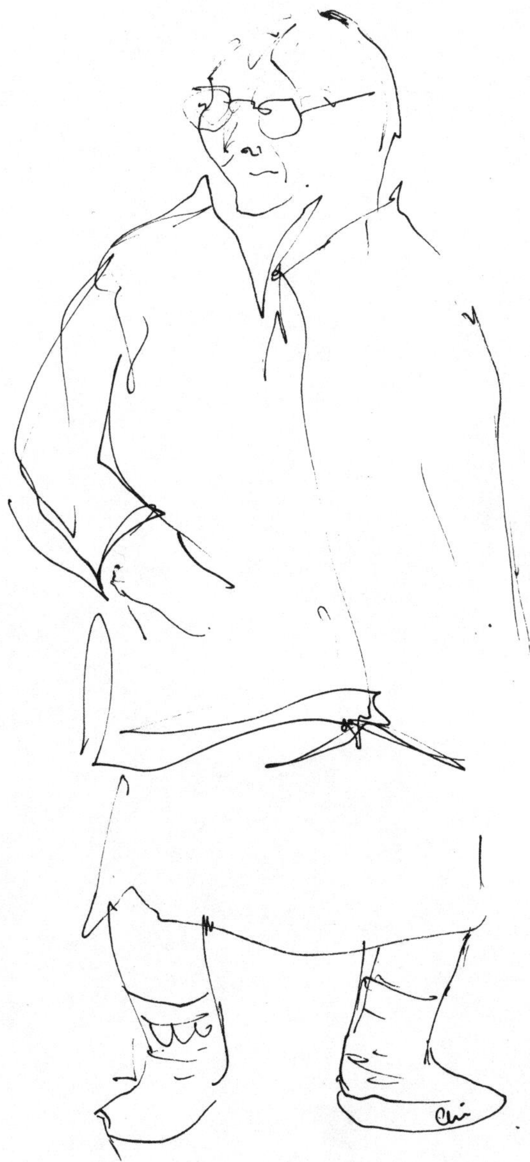

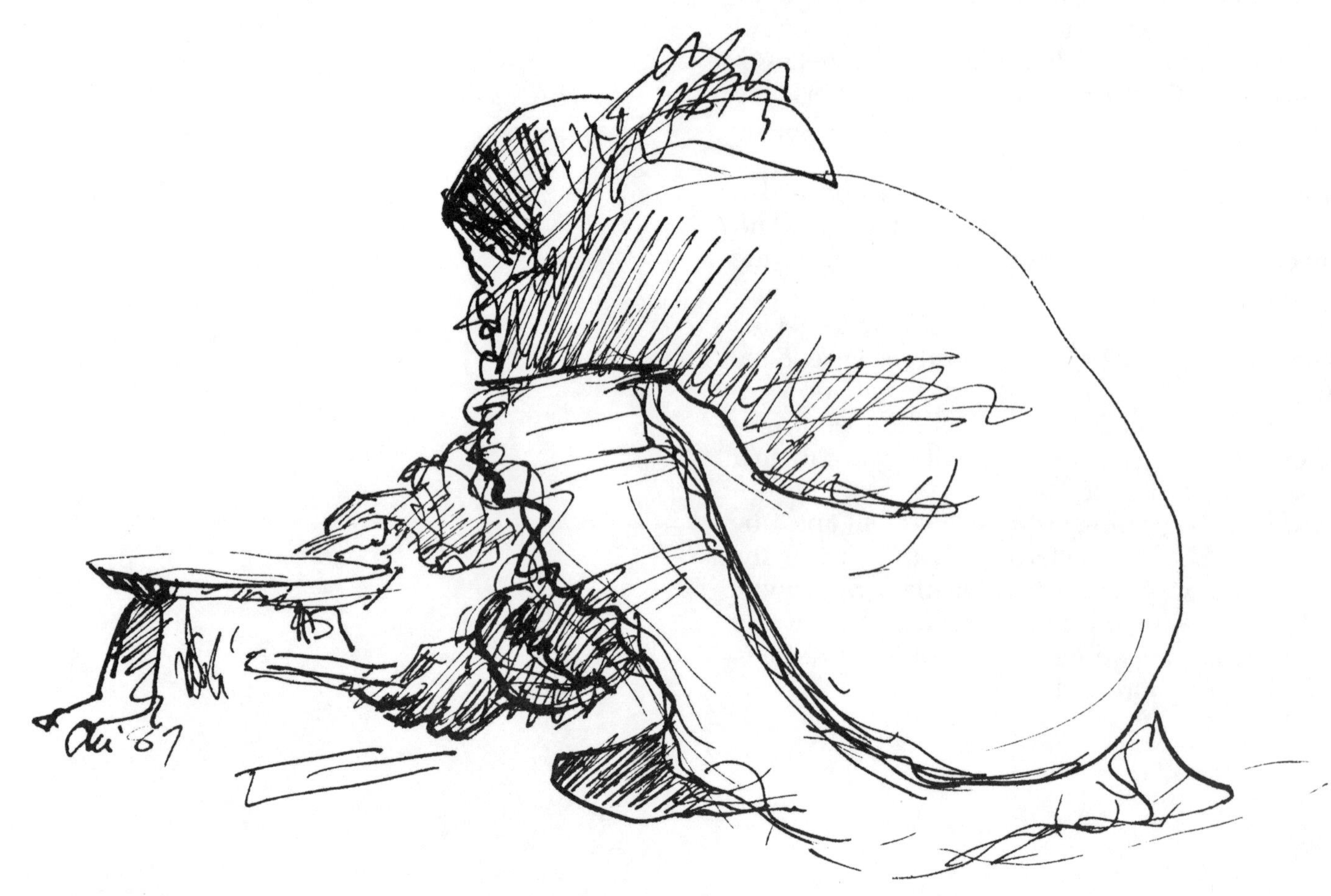

3rd August

The demon wind is king. Within the green cave of my tent, I can hear it coming, screaming across the tundra like a banshee, until it slams against the walls and snaps and flaps them like a badly trimmed sail. The frame rocks and trembles, and I wonder if the splint, and humming, quivering rigging will hold the broken pole. Pinpricks of light shine through a constellation of holes where the canvas has worn thin, and needles of icy rain rattle against the roof and seep through the walls to collect in puddles on the floor. It is the middle of the day, but I huddle in my sleeping bag in the driest spot I can find and try to stay warm.

I am camped beyond the fishing village at West Arm. Through the slit that appears sporadically in the billowing door, I see a flat, grey bay, hissing with whitecaps, from which most of the ice has been driven. Yesterday, sluggish floes still ground against the beach, and, further towards town, rafts of ice touched the shore and people stood on them and jigged for char through the gaps. In town, the ice went out two weeks ago.

I had fish for breakfast, cooked on a tin plate over a driftwood fire, but there was much more than I could eat, and the rest lies under a flat stone, hidden from the gulls. Tomati gave me the fish. He and Joseph caught fifty last

Stalks horizontal in rosette form
Slightly bristly. Sepals bristly & with
little leaf at base!

Grows in such profusion at end
July that whole tundra smells
of it!
Roots & flowers edible

<u>YELLOW OXYTROPE</u>.
Oxytropis Maydelliana

night in a net not far from my tent. One end of the net is anchored to a rock so close to the shore that it is exposed in the barely noticeable tide which now rises and falls. Although they are closely related to Pacific salmon, char do not die when they spawn, and they are now running back out to sea. The sleek, powerful fish come into the shallows after little grey shrimp, and hundreds of these translucent crustaceans spilled over my wind-numbed fingers when I gutted the fish at the edge of the sea.

When Tomati and his friend first strung the net, slabs of ice threatened to tear it away, and the men jumped from floe to floe and pushed them apart with poles. But when the wind changed, and the ice blew out to sea, they pulled a canoe along the net and tossed the heavy, convulsing bodies into the boat behind them. They would freeze some, and the rest would dry, orange-fleshed, on racks around their houses. Once they caught a loon which had drowned in the net, and which they said was good to eat.

While we waited for the net to fill again, we walked across the tundra. The northern oxytrope, a member of the pea family, was blooming in great profusion. Tomati told me that it was edible, and we stuffed bunches of the yellow flowers into our mouths, but they tasted like grass clippings, and I did not like them much. I found out later, after I had returned to the south, that these are related to locoweed, which is poisonous, so it was perhaps just as well I did not eat too many. We also plucked the small fat leaves of the arctic sorrel, and they are very tart and delicious, like rhubarb.

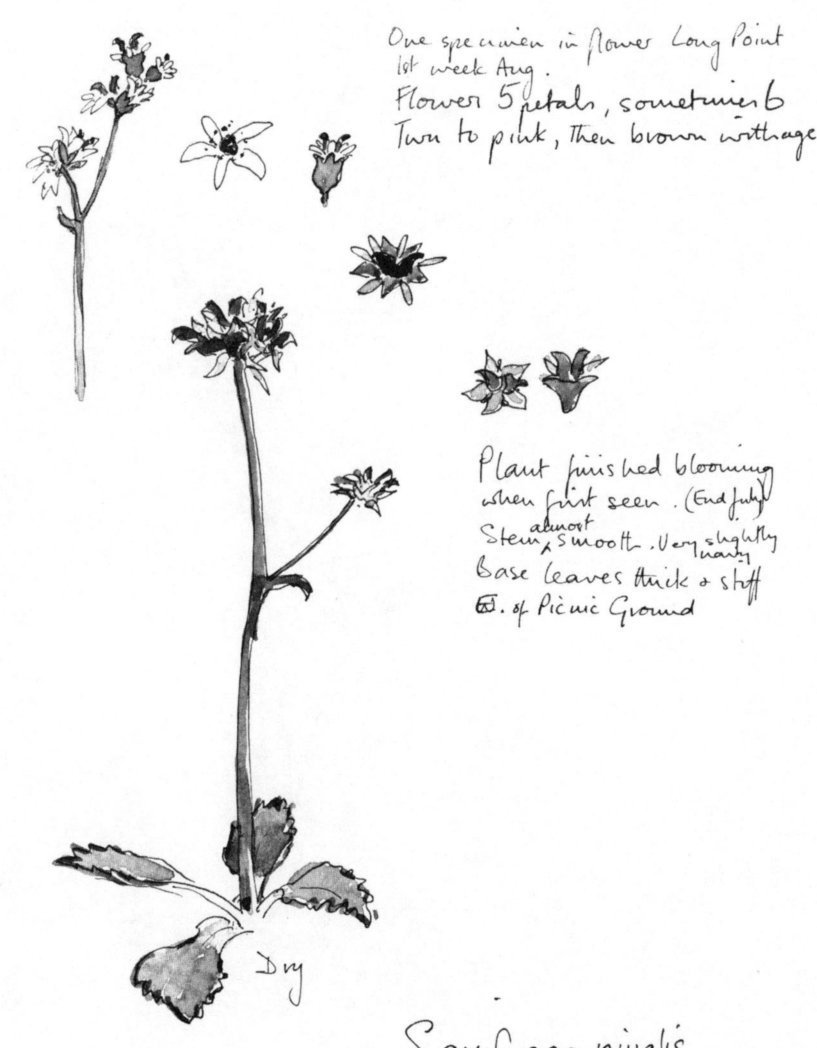

One specimen in flower Long Point
1st week Aug.
Flower 5 petals, sometimes 6
Turn to pink, then brown with age

Plant finished blooming
when first seen . (End July)
      almost
Stem ˄ smooth . Very slightly
                        many
Base leaves thick & stiff
E. of Picnic Ground

Dry

Saxifraga nivalis

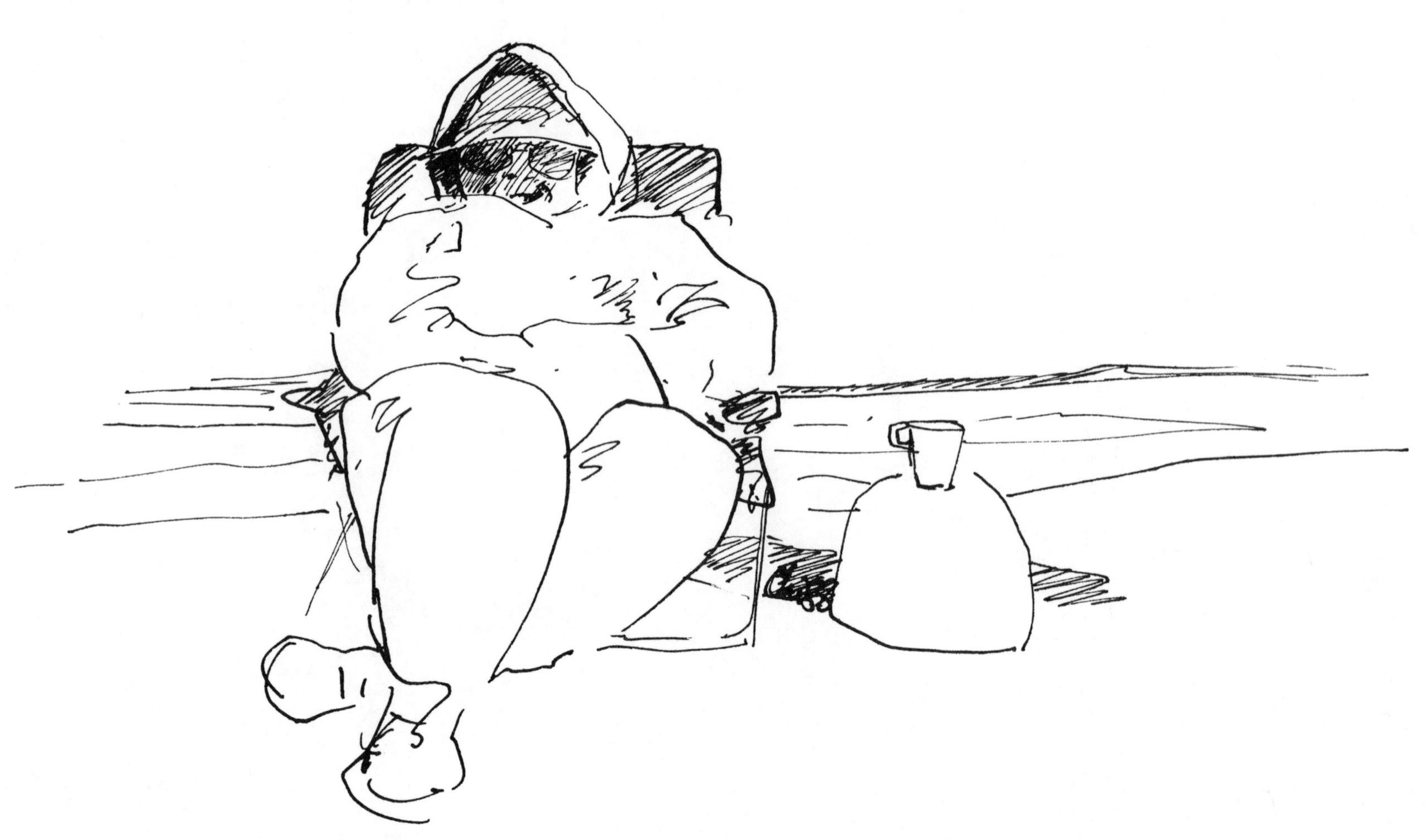

6th August

Yesterday was my birthday and it snowed. Strangely, it did not seem cold, for there was not much wind. The thick, soft flakes dissolved into the mud and did not settle.

I had left my camp to the vagaries of the weather and hitchhiked back to town, to say goodbye to Katie's mother, who was due to fly out on the "redeye special" at 2 A.M. this morning, one of the three planes a week to the outside. But when she and her family arrived at the airport in a borrowed truck, they found the place deserted and a notice tacked to the door saying the flight had been cancelled. No one had thought to phone the would-be travellers. Katie's mother was astonished to find the swings and slides behind the school in full use, at 2 A.M., with the sleet driving past in gusts. School starts in a couple of weeks, and the kids will have a hard time readjusting to a time schedule. Katie's boy has sometimes been up for twenty-four hours at a stretch, then sleeps for seventeen.

20th August

Has it really been so long since I last wrote? Time is racing.

I come and go occasionally to my camp, but whereas, when I first came here I camped five days and stayed in town for two, now it is the other way round. My tent has had the biscuit. It became as full of holes as a colander, and finally ripped up one side, but Katie and Dennis have put theirs up right by the sea not far from where mine used to be, and I use it now. It stands swaybacked in the wind — but at least it stands.

It has been the wettest summer that anyone can remember. July had four inches of rain when it should have been totally dry (and in an area where annual precipitation should only be ten inches, that is a lot). So far, during August, it has either rained or snowed to some degree on every single day.

Susan Mackay was due home, and I needed to find another place to live (although, in fact, she did not come back when expected, and I continued to go over every few days to water the plants). I made arrangements to use Tomati's house while he went to a conference in Yellowknife. The house was a godsend. It was down by the waterfront in a much quieter part of town, and through the window I could see nothing but the sea and sky separated by a thin sliver of land. It is at the end of a block of units, so I have only one neighbour, and he is hardly ever at home.

Tomati is an interesting man. He is from Pelly Bay, a community strong on native tradition, and he has striven to maintain the dignity of his people by fostering that tradition and yet adapting successfully to the demands and influences of the Canadian government. He was with the North West Territories booth at Expo '86 in Vancouver, and he was one of the drum dancers at the Northern Games. It is his picture that I have drawn.

Rosemary, his wife, comes from the south. She has an arts degree, and one of her photographs is hanging on the wall. It is of an inukshuk, a stone man, silhouetted against a sunset, and the simple black rock shapes fill the frame like the brushstrokes of a Chinese character. Rosemary has adapted to the Inuit way. Her tasks are with the house and children, of which they have three. Time means nothing, and she must be prepared to feed her family or visitors at any hour of the day, and obey her husband in such matters without hesitation. It is not considered degrading to do this. Each member of an Inuit partnership is of equal importance, but their roles are fairly rigid. Rosemary's husband is a good provider, and that is his job. The freezer is full of meat and fish (and fur mitts and boots of uncured skins which are stored there for the summer), and cariboo skin parkas hang in the porch. A child's parka has been beautifully fashioned from the skin of a young cariboo. The top of the hood is formed by the animal's face. The eyes have been sewn shut, but the ears remain erect, peeking up above the child's own ears. Cariboo skin sheds fiercely, and every time I brush against the parkas in the porch, white tubular hairs stick to my clothes.

And suddenly, now that the town no longer crowds and cramps, I can paint. Apart from a few black and white sketches, and the flower drawings, I have been unable to do anything so far. At camp, when the sun shone and the

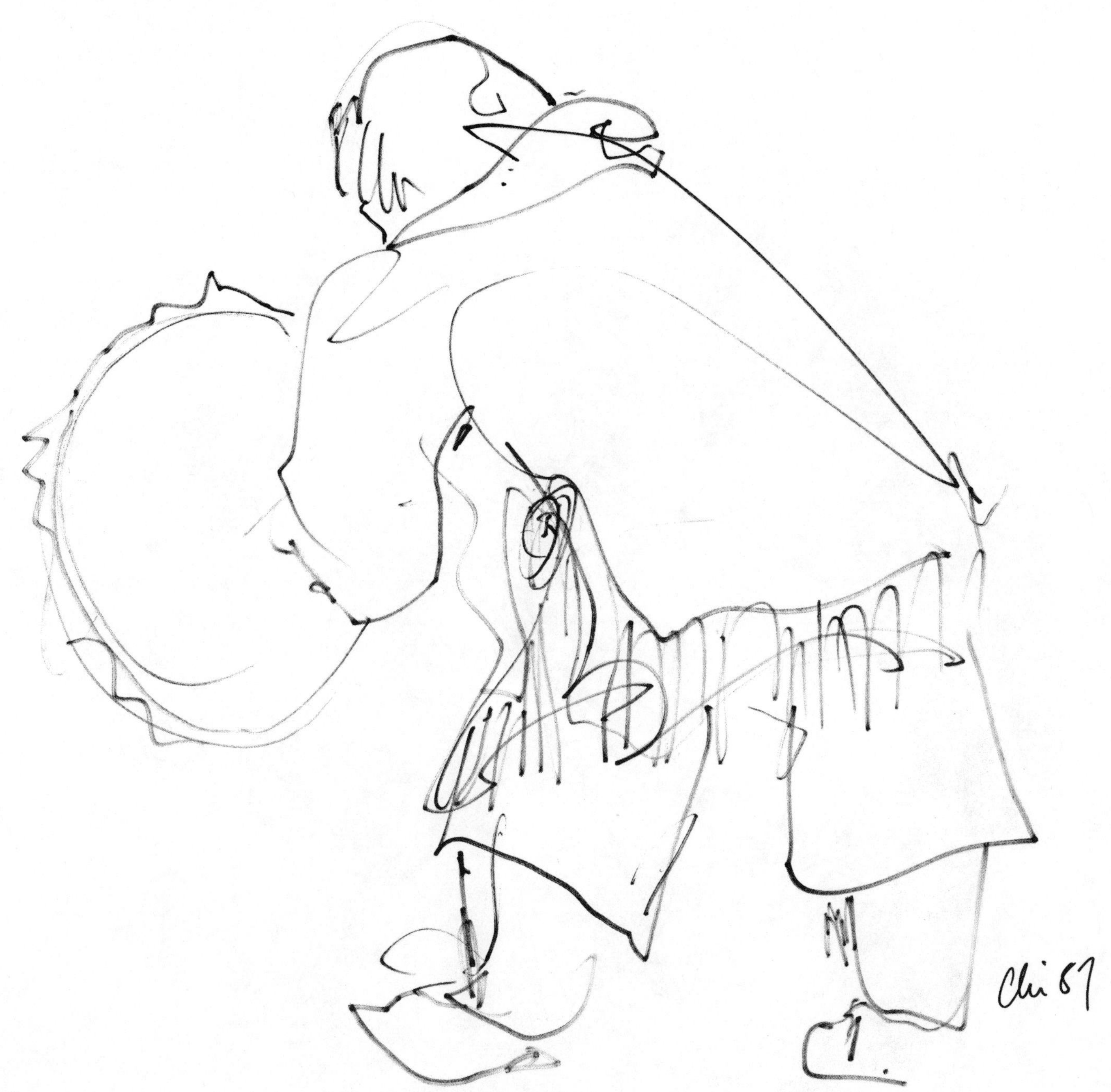

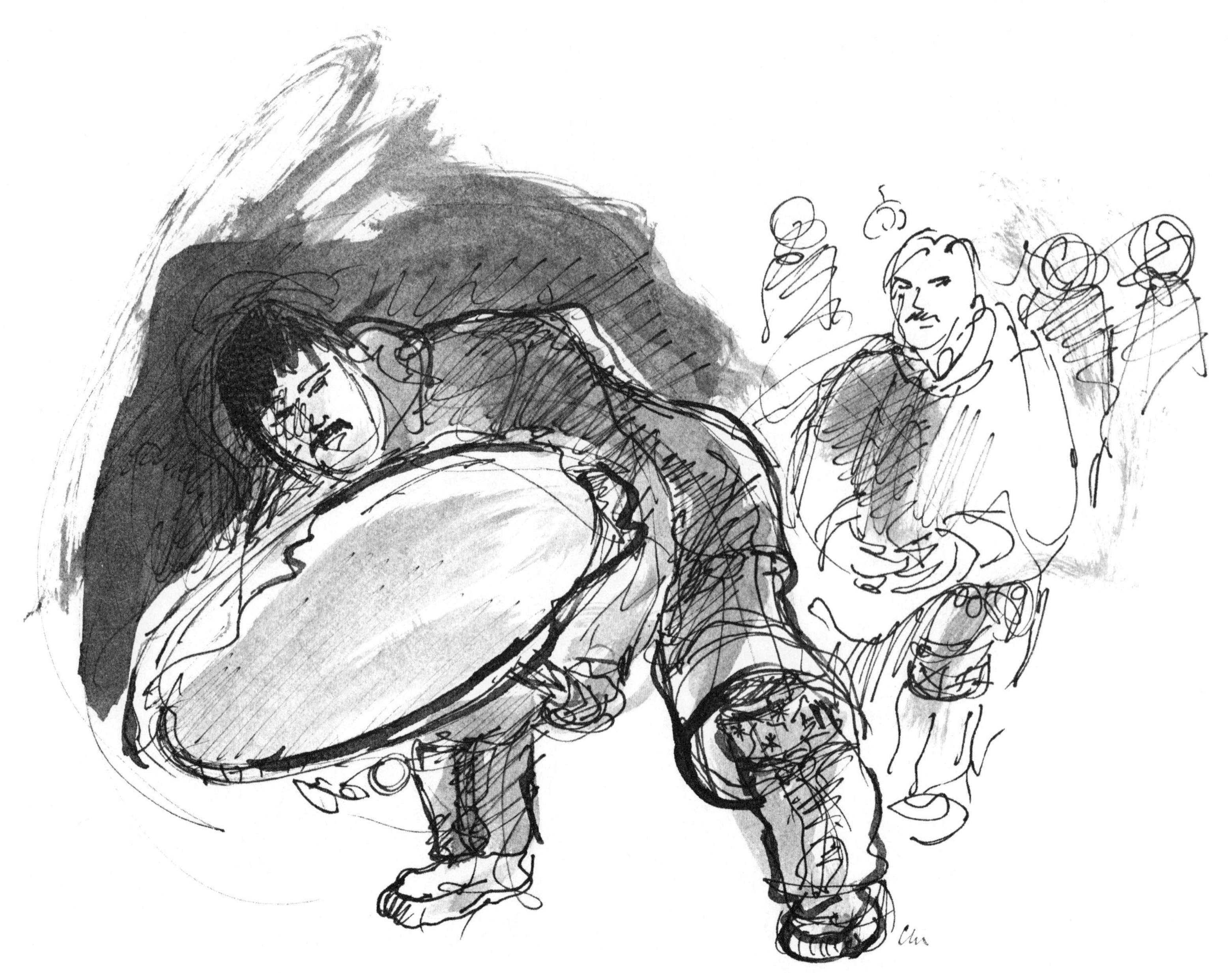

wind was not at its wildest, the glare on the paper was prohibitive. Inside the tent, the only shade, the green, filtered light, obliterated colours. And in rain, of course, it was impossible. At least, these were my excuses. How can I interpret the lightness, the paleness, the shapelessness of the landscape and still convey the brutality and harshness? All compositions revolve around a flat horizontal at the bottom of the paper. As time marches, I become panicky: have I lost that elusive flame of creativity? Have I become impotent?

But it is always the same when I come to a new environment. For weeks, the spirit of the place eludes me, and I bog down with banal trivialities, producing surface images at which the non-initiated look and say, "Oh, isn't that nice!" but which leave me cringing with shame for myself and disgust at their lack of sensitivity. An unreasonable attitude perhaps, but one I cannot escape.

The Arctic, however, must have smouldered quietly within me, like the little driftwood fires that burned invisibly until the wind came, and now, without thought, I state the landscape's emptiness by painting skies. I paint the boiling, streaking, freckling, ripping, shattering clouds as they roll and tumble past the window. My brush shoves and batters, jabs and splatters, driven by the urgency of the wind. Often, though, the clouds are flat and grey, and then I sit against the sky-filled window, close to the rain-scribbled glass, and read. The back door does not close tightly, and the wind whines a maniacal dirge through the crack.

The evening of the tenth stands out in my memory because the weather broke. The clouds fell apart, the wind dropped, and the sun shone. The calm was unnerving. For so long, one's body had been braced to meet the roar and batter of the wind, that when it stopped, there was nothing more to lean against, and it was like falling into a void. One walked uncertainly, expecting another onslaught, unable to relax when it did not come.

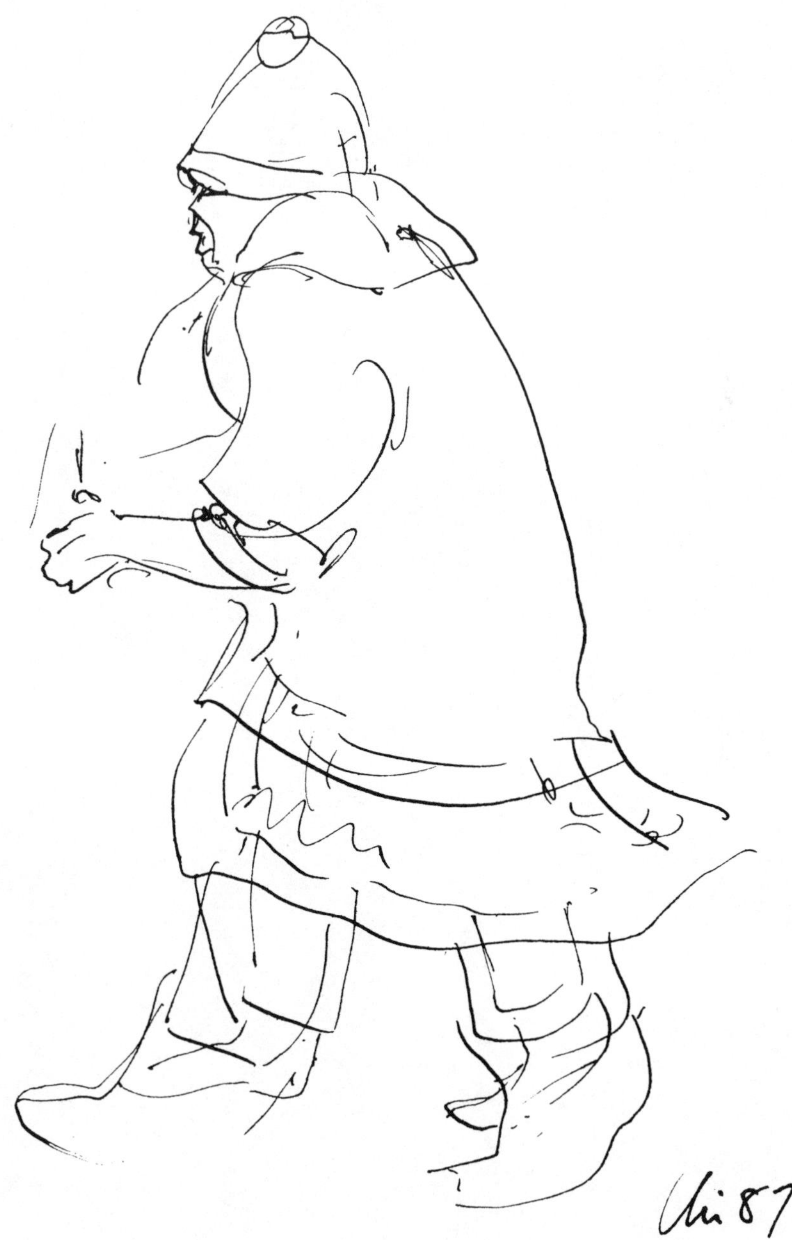

The sun has begun to set for an hour or two at night, although the light still barely dims, and when the weather cleared, it stood low to the north, and ruddy. Colours jumped up vividly. And into the harbour, into the frame of my window, came a ship.

She was large and squat, with a tall, boxlike superstructure, a massive funnel and a strong hull painted the vivid red of the Coast Guard vessels. She steamed slowly into the bay, glowing like a fireball in the last of the sunlight. Her anchor chain rattled into the water. She was the George R. Pearkes, she was an icebreaker, and she heralded the arrival of the barge.

Since the MacKenzie River opened in May, fleets of barges have ferried freight to Tuktoyoktuk, a journey of about nine days from the end of the road at Hay River. As soon as the ice permitted, they braved the Arctic Sea. A tug pulled them in a long line through the ocean, but as she steamed through the heads, she marshalled her flock into a raft and pushed them slowly towards the wharf.

The barges were great, flat slabs of hollow iron, filled with fuel below, with the rest of the freight lashed on top. I had thought that the orange boxes stacked on deck were packing cases, until the barges docked and then the crates were revealed as full-sized truck containers. What had appeared to be a small tank, like a boiler, became an enormous fuel reservoir many stories high. Beside it, a van and three new pickups looked like children's toys. The barges carried their own giant forklift tractors, with wheels as tall as a man.

There was much excitement with this invasion (on how the kids regretted starting school!). Several people in town had grocery orders from the south to try and combat the exorbitant prices charged in the stores. But the bulk of the freight was fuel, and much of the rest was building supplies. Most arctic communities are expanding rapidly, now that people no longer live as nomads and the survival rate of children has dramatically increased. Nine houses

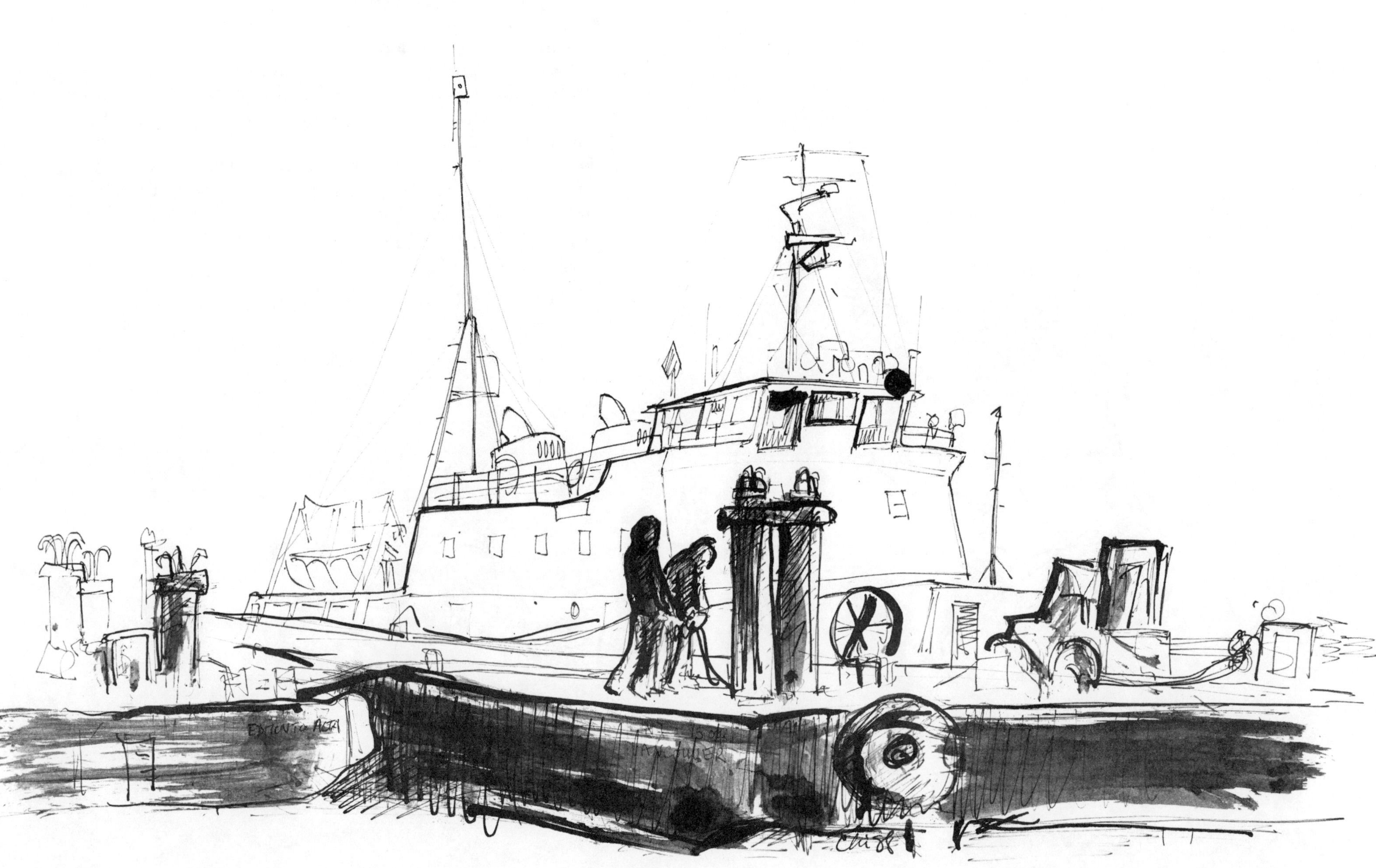

and a new community centre are expected to be habitable by Christmas. Teams of construction workers will come up from the south and work twelve or fourteen hours a day until they are completed.

Now, the giant tractors roared and beeped along the narrow muddy roads through town, and orange containers and piles of lumber and insulation sprang up like mushrooms. The crew was a friendly bunch, and they dished out frisbees and footballs to excited children and, when they were not too busy, gave us tours of the boat. Unlike the occupants of the icebreaker, which limited their hospitality to cocktail parties by invitation only.

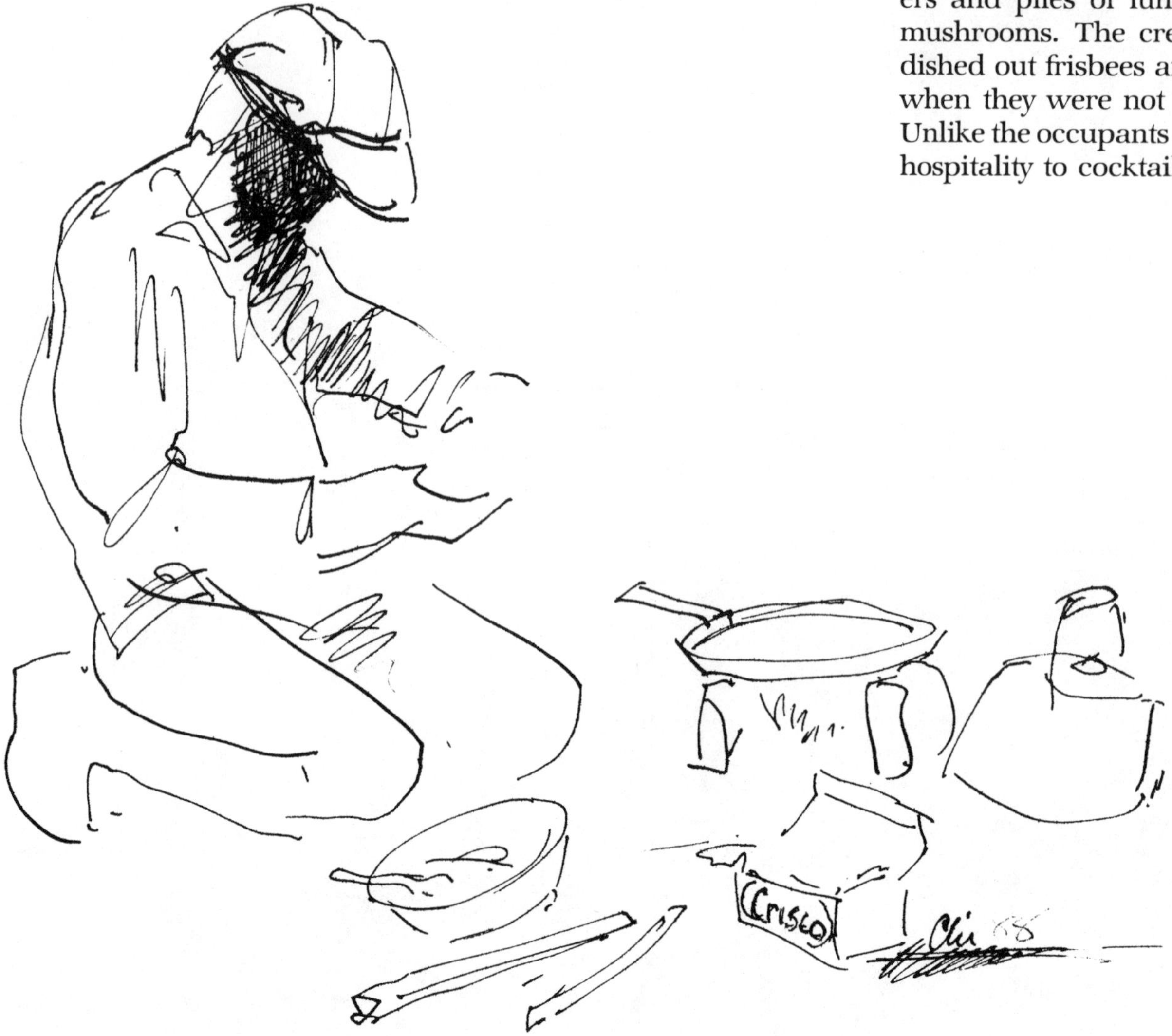

Many visitors had come to town during the summer. They had flown in and out and made very little impression on the rhythms of people's lives. But the ships were different. They had travelled on the surface of the earth and broached the isolation in a way that a plane could never do. They had joined this tight, ugly cluster of buildings to the rest of Canada.

By far the most interesting vessel to glide within the frame of my window was a yacht. It came hard on the heels of the icebreaker; it was the last thing I would have expected to see up here. But, I learned, there were three or four sailing craft attempting to travel the Northwest Passage. Two boys had got as far as Cambridge Bay last summer in a Hobi Cat, and they had headed east from here at the end of July this year, hoping to be the first to complete the passage powered by sail alone. The twin hulls of their specially strengthened catamaran had a small deck, but no cabin. Their only shelter was the insulated wetsuits they wore, and a tent for the times they could not travel. If the weather was fit, they sailed, no matter how many hours they had to stay awake. When they hit ice, they dragged the boat over it.

The yacht, the Belvedere, was essentially motor powered despite its tall, graceful masts. It was a luxurious boat, large, with sophisticated computers and radar equipment, and much cabin space. I presented myself on board at once, consumed with curiosity. I was given coffee, and when I could ignore the sly and sickening lurch, as the boat bumped about beside the dock (for the wind was once more howling like a dervish from the north), I found myself among a group of very fascinating people.

The owner was John Bockstoce, a big, lively man, forty-three, who has poured his enormous energies into researching the history of whaling. He has written several books. This was his twenty-sixth summer in the Arctic and the second year that he had attempted the Northwest Passage in the Belvedere. He had once completed it in a walrus skin umiak, a type of craft which is still used among some of the native communities in Alaska. It had been equipped with an outboard motor (as they all are these days) and tents and radios, but the ice was still the ice, and the journey had taken three years.

Sven, the skipper, had been part of John's crew for many years. He was short and barrel-like, with a grizzled beard, a squeaky voice, and a strong Swedish accent. Mark, a cabinetmaker from Vancouver Island, was the exact opposite. He was very tall, thin, and almost painfully quiet. He was an experienced sailor but new to this boat, as was Judy, from Massachusets, a thirty-nine-year old marine biologist who ran a consulting firm and did some teaching. Bonnie was the cook. She had known Sven and John for years, and two of her sons had been on the Umiak expedition. She had lived all her life in Alaska by the Bering Sea, and had wonderful stories. Like how she had raised a polar bear cub in her house, like a dog, and how, when she had lived with her husband in the native community of Wainwrite, her husband had fired the fatal shot that had killed a grey whale and had thus been offered the most favoured part, the fin. Bonnie said she popped a bit in her mouth, and it was just like a rubber band, but she was determined not to give up, and twenty-four hours later, she was still chewing. When she moved to Nome, a beluga whale washed up on her beach, and stunk the place out for weeks. So when, one moonlit night, she saw another bobbing in with the tide, she swam out to it to push it away, but found it was the body of a man, floating face down. She dragged him, face down, in the moonlight, above the reach of the tide, and went to phone the police. The first thing they asked her was: "Has the man a glass eye?"

And into this melting pot of extraordinary people came Carl, a Norwegian in this sixties, with a tanned face and thick, white hair. He had sailed around the world single-handed, had skied alone across the Greenland icecap, and, this year, had kayaked down the MacKenzie River with a friend, then east along the coast until time and weather had forced his friend to turn back. Carl had hitched a ride with the pilot from the float plane base to Cambridge Bay, arriving just in time to beg passage on the Belvedere for the rest of her voyage.

The Nahidik, the buoy tender, came hard on the Belvedere's heels. The crews knew each other, for all the boats were following close against the ice. The Captain invited us back on board his ship to enjoy the hot tub which the crew had built on the upper deck. We climbed to the bridge, festooned the radar gear with our clothes, rushed across the icy deck which was higher than any of the Guildings in town, and gave us a marvelous view, and sat there, cooking from the neck down, with the wind and dusk and rain beating about our heads. I have rarely been in a more unlikely situation.

The next day, the wind lessened and a drizzle set in. The Belvedere steamed away. All the ships have reported bad ice out to sea, especially to the east of us, between Cambridge Bay and Pelly Bay. It doesn't sound too promising for the Belvedere. I wish them well.

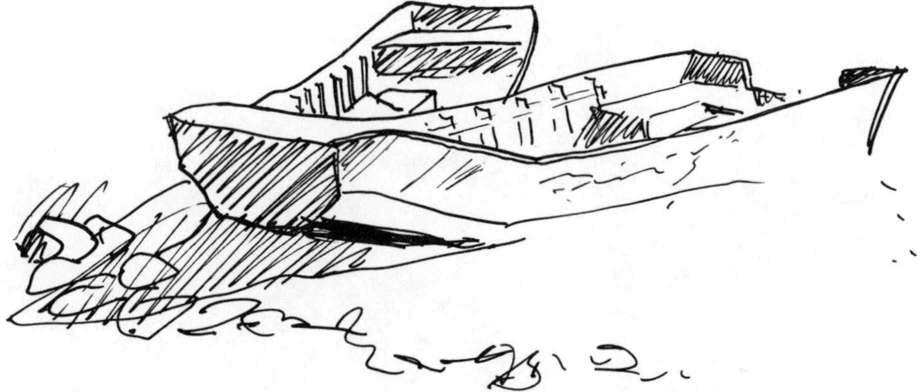

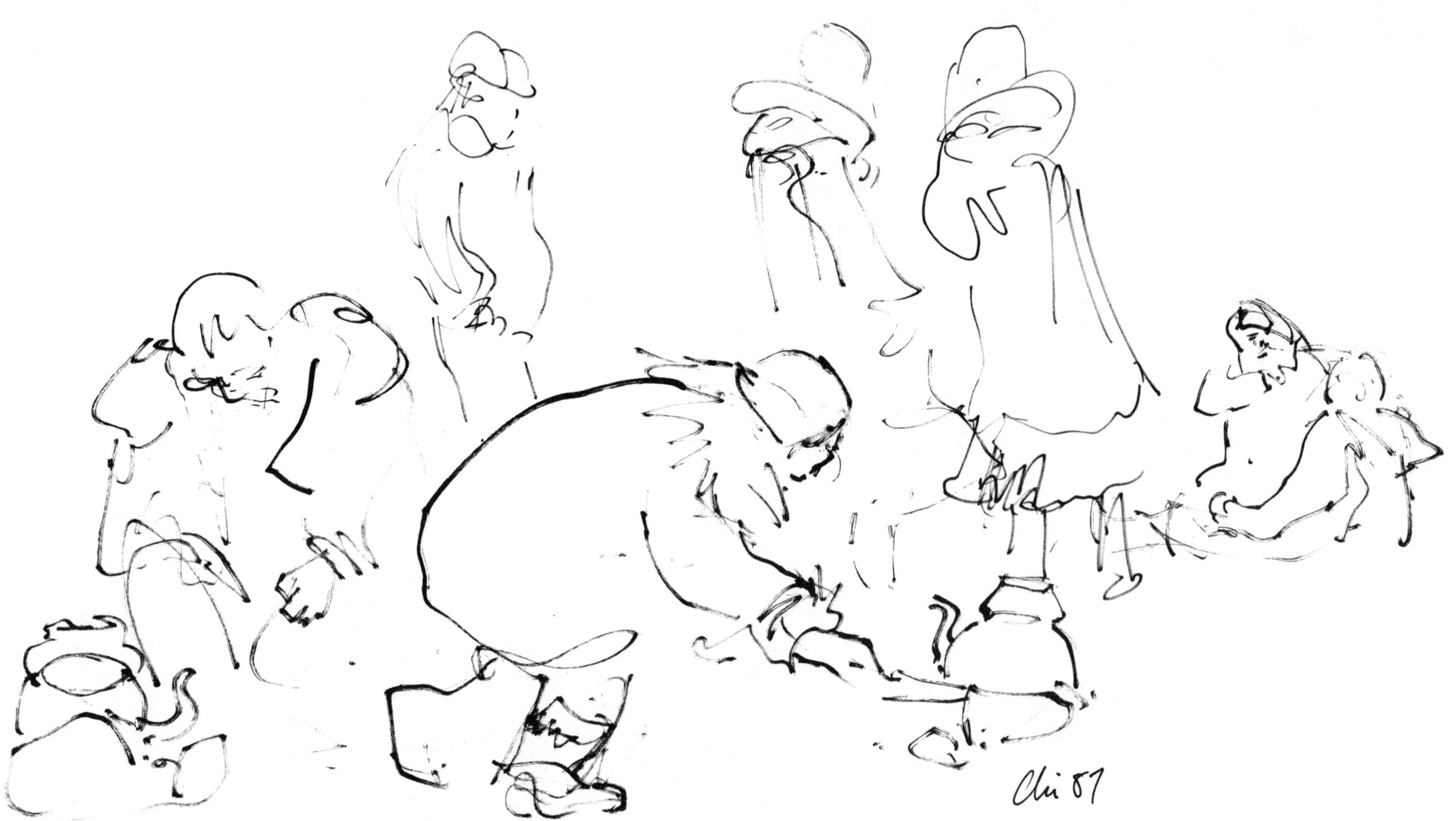

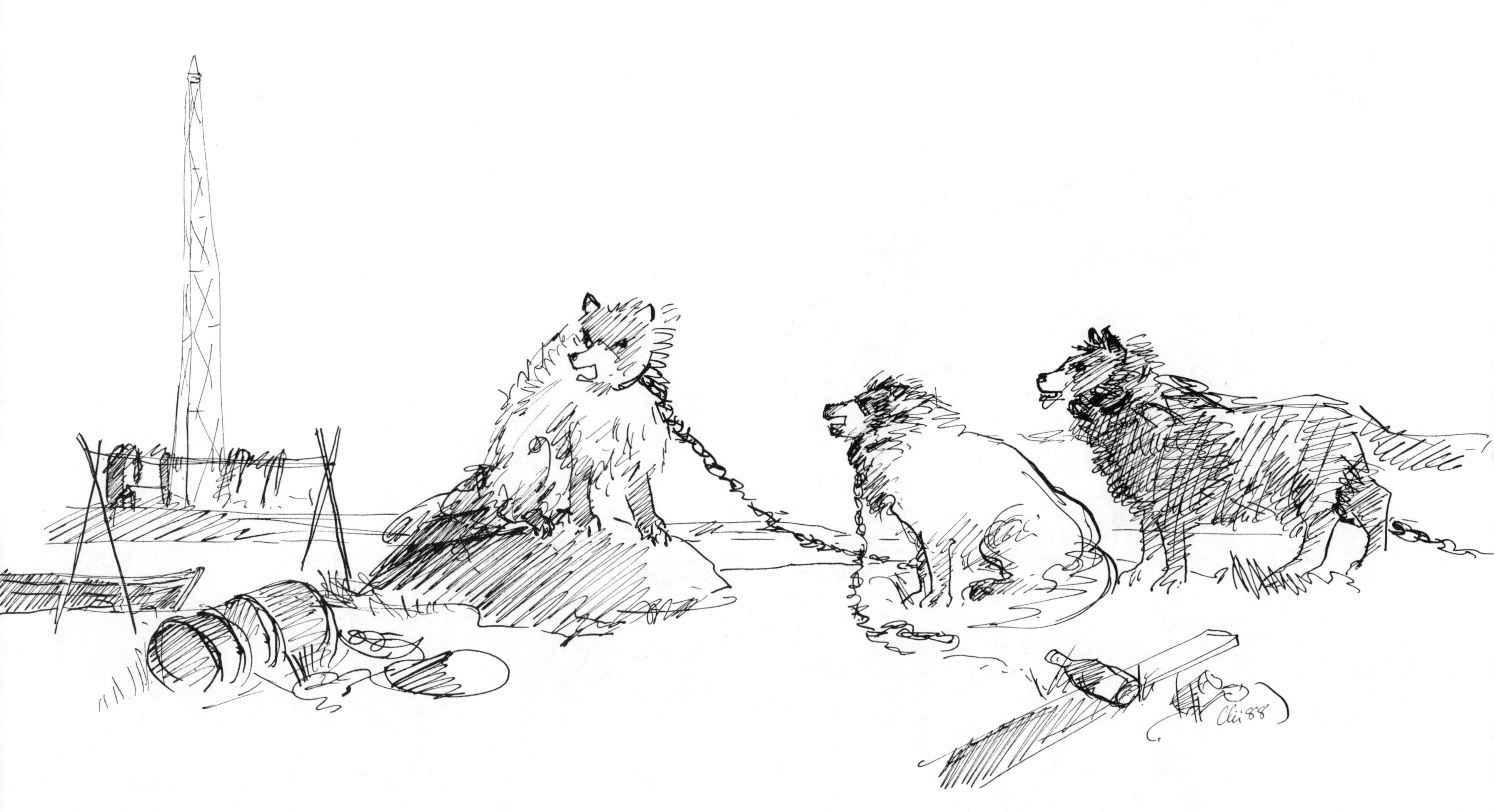

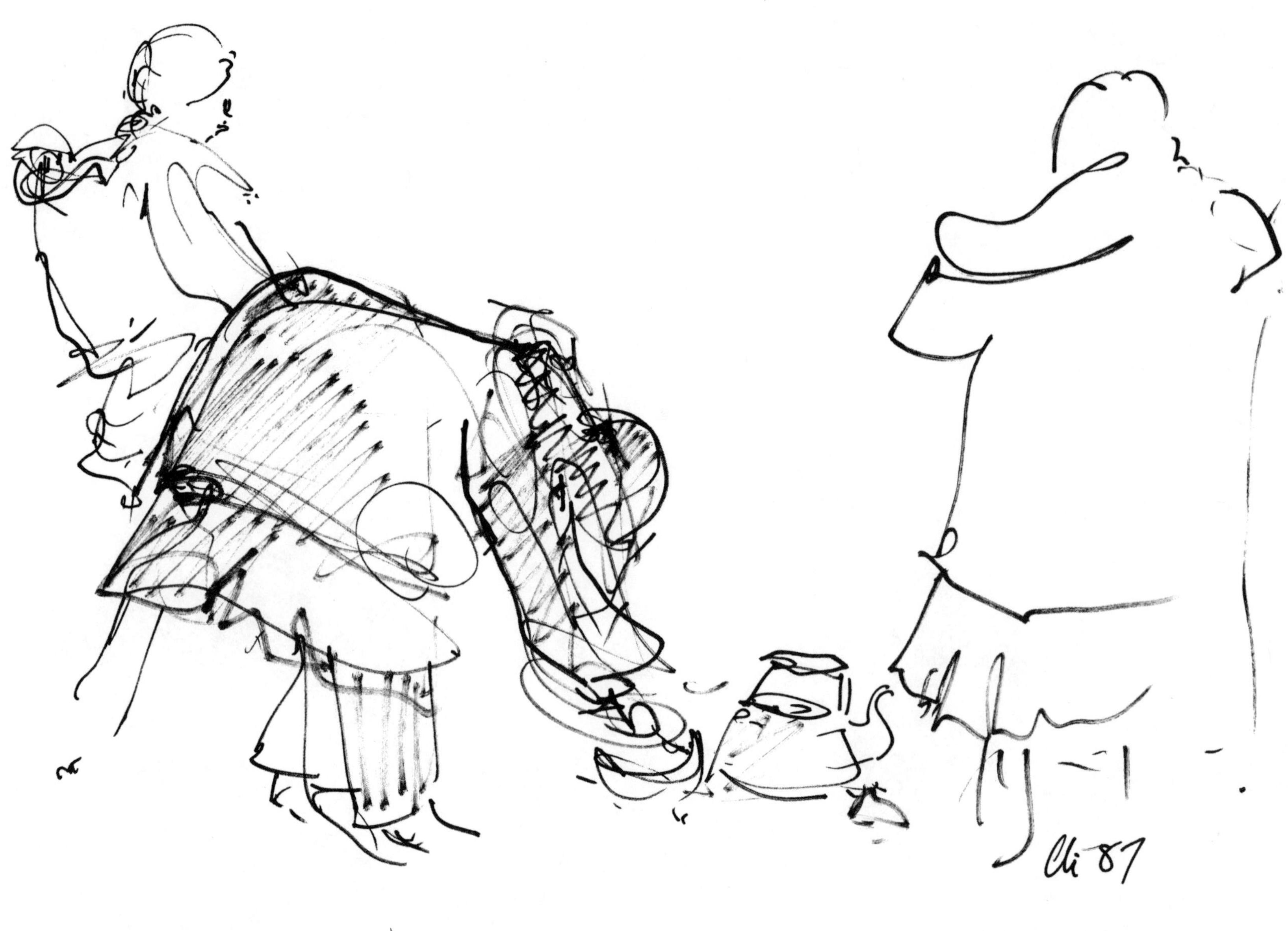

When school started, Susan Mackay came home. She was not, as I had thought, a white person, or kabloona, who had gone to the south for her vacation, but an Inuk, who had been visiting her people far to the north in Resolute Bay. I had been guilty of the grossest of all crimes, stereotyping. I had assumed that, because Susan read "Chatelaine" and enjoyed valentine cards, she must be white. Mary, like so many of her people, had simply blended the best of the old world with the conveniences of the new. It explained the preponderance of meat knives and lack of bread utensils in the kitchen — meat would be a predominant part of the diet and also the fact that she had adopted a child later in life, for that is a common custom among the Inuit. And now that I have met the little blond-haired boy, I see his eyes are slightly slanting, and he, too, is of mixed heritage.

Not everyone has made the transition so smoothly. Some have been swept into the vicious circle of alcohol and drug abuse. Many settlements are dry, but Cambridge Bay allowed beer in on the Friday plane. It was subsidized and, at a dollar a can, was the cheapest drink on the place (milk was five dollars a quart), and sold at the Hudson's Bay Company store. The lineup on Friday nights straggled across the neighbouring waste lot. Not everyone who bought booze abused it, of course, but it was distressing to see those who did. Some were well-educated people with high government positions. It saddened many of the Inuit who saw their traditional values disintegrating.

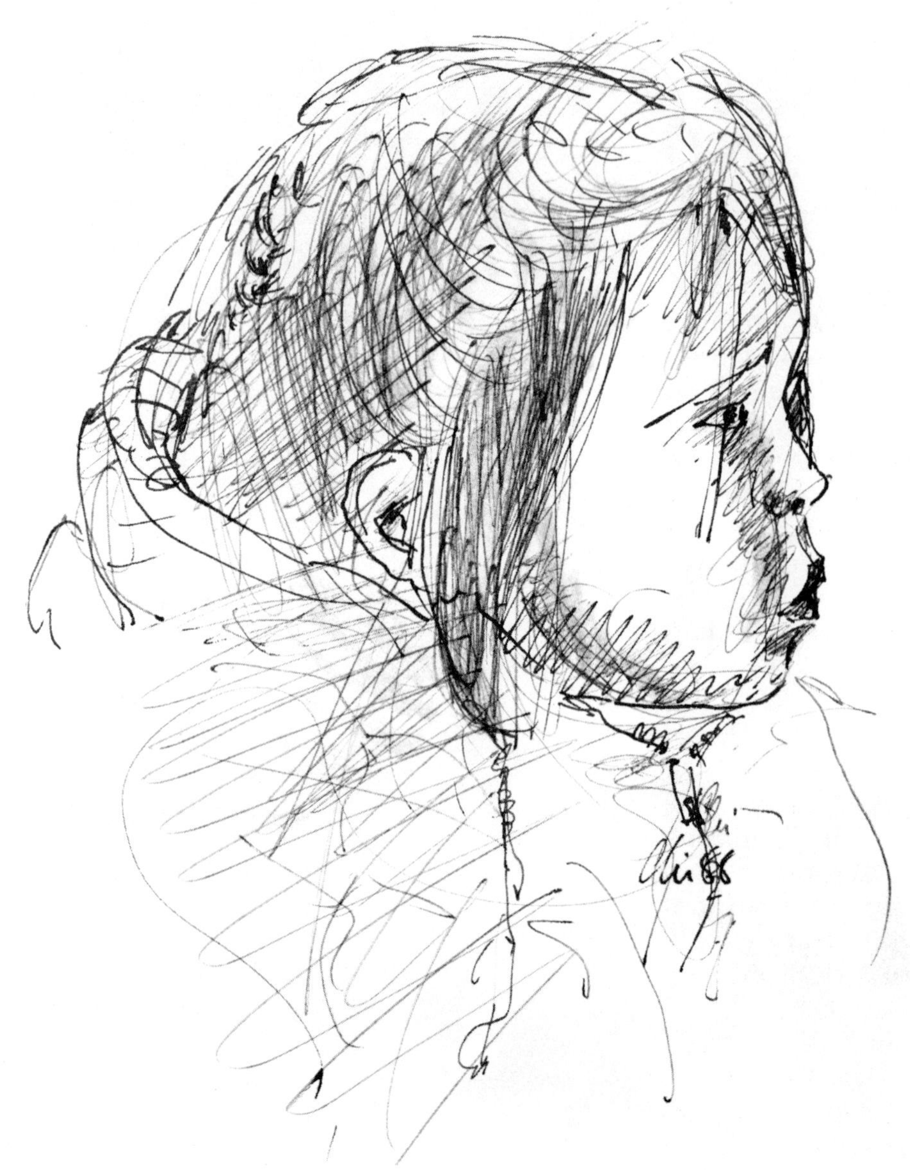

26th August

There are four hours of semi-darkness now, and the sun sets twelve minutes earlier each day. I have become so used to the daylight that, while watching the news from the south, on the TV in Tomati's house, it came as something of a shock to remember that the rest of the world has night.

We've had better weather this last week. There has been less wind, and sometimes the sun has shone for the whole day. Some of the men from town went over to the mainland, a four-hour journey by powerboat, wind permitting, to hunt cariboo. They were lucky, and got back within three days; often the wind traps them down there. They had shot seven animals, and the meat hangs in dark slabs over the drying racks. I know some of these people now, like Luke Toodlik. He is a small, tidy man married to a girl from Ontario. They have a bewitching three year old with ivory skin and coal black eyes and hair. There is some conflict about the child's upbringing; Janie tries to maintain some white discipline, and Luke indulges his daughter in the Inuit way. In the house, one of the few in the settlement that is privately owned, is the biggest colour T.V. I have ever seen. You have to sit at the furthermost corner of the room to look at it. Janie says Luke wants a bigger one yet.

I hiked to Mt. Pelly yesterday, squinting into the glare of an early sun, and the tundra was green and bright and unfamiliar without its usual overcast. Water glistened everywhere — the country has grown wetter instead of drying out as it should — for the permafrost has not allowed the rain to drain away. The mats of arctic willow, which had been leafless and fuzzy with flowers when I came here two months ago, are now fluffy with seed. The greylag geese have gathered in clamouring flocks, and they will leave and begin their journey south in a few days.

The wind freshened as the sun rose higher, but it was not particularly cold as long as I kept moving, and I climbed the ancient beaches where the sea had pounded 10,000 years ago, and plodded up the long, slow slope to the summit. A young fox, gangly, looselimbed, loped along the crest. Up there, the wind was squeezed and concentrated by the bulge in the landscape, and it slammed into my clothing and wrenched my hair so that I felt that, if I stretched my arms, I would lift off the ground and soar across the web of land with its glittering, wind-scoured pools, far into the empty distance and round the very curve of the earth.

A pair of rough-legged hawks hung below the summit. They had a nest on the steeper, eastern slope of the mountain. It was an amazing piece of engineering, a massive platform of willow twigs that must have taken generations to build. The willow bushes were common enough in the swamps, although there were none close to the nest, but they grew and disintegrated extremely slowly. Dead wood was rare, and the willow's stringy fibres made it difficult to break off. There must have been thousands of branches in the nest.

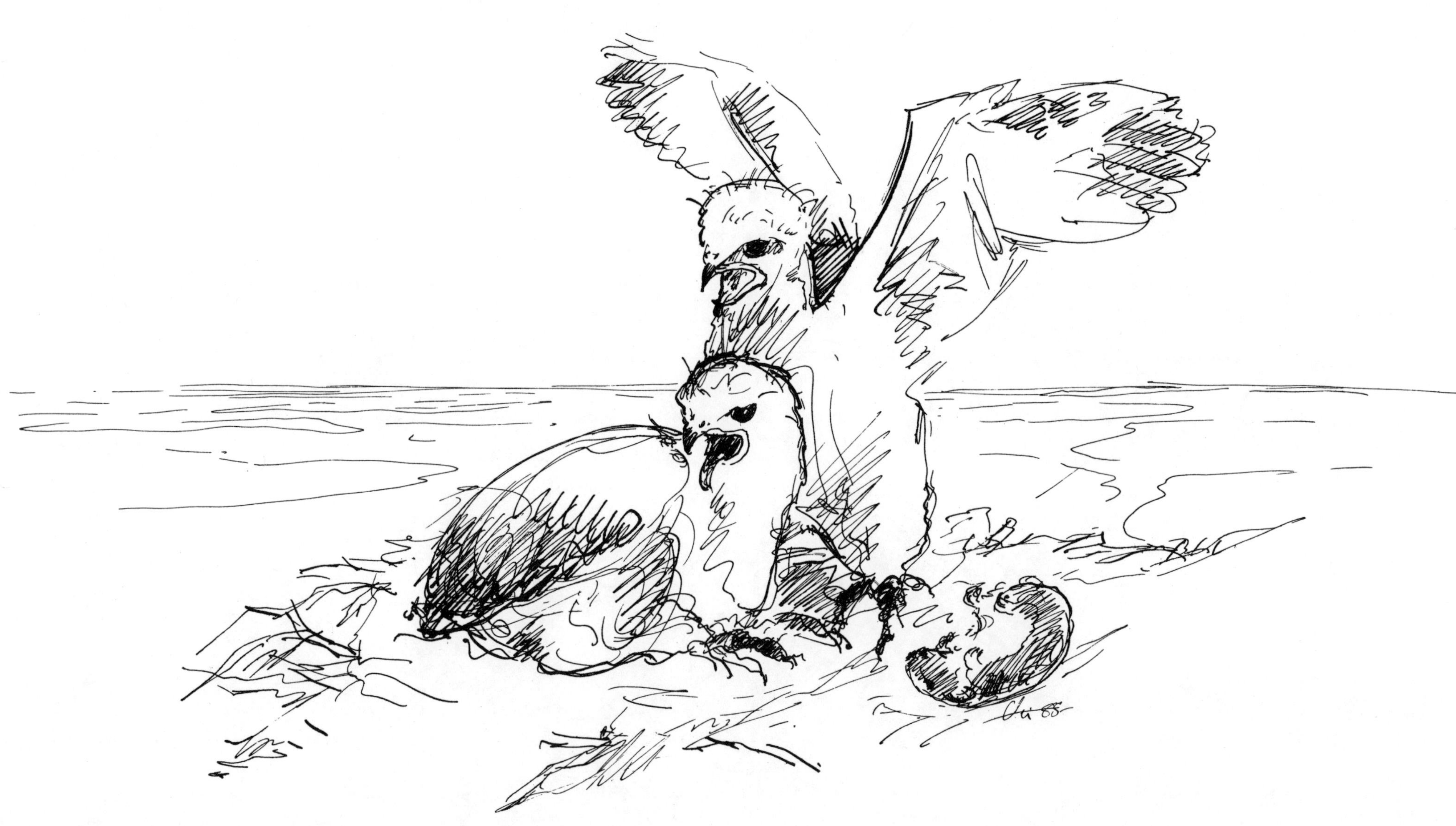

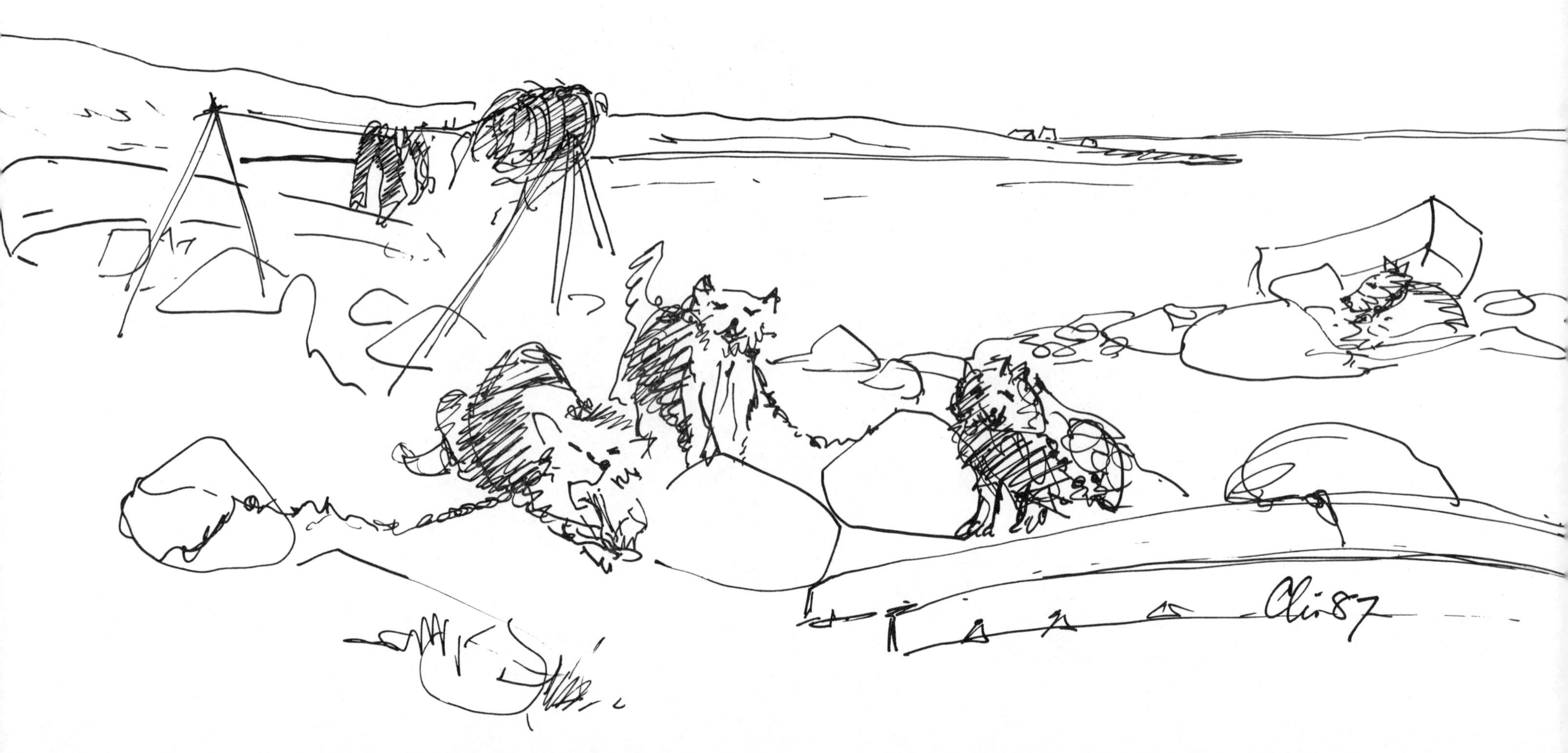

The slope was loose and soft with rain, but it was possible to slither down to the platform. I had first seen it three weeks before, when the babies were newly hatched and covered with silvery down. Now two of them were half fledged, and they hissed malevolently at me with gaping beaks and fierce hawk's eyes. Their yellow feet were well formed with large, sharp claws, but to me, this show of bravado looked a little ridiculous, for their beaks were edged with fat, yellow baby lips, and wayward pieces of fluff sprouted charmingly from between the half-formed adult feathers.

The third fledgling was much smaller and poorly developed. He gaped instinctively when I went to close, but he could not lift his head, and his aggressive siblings sat on him. There had originally been four eggs, but only two fledglings would reach maturity. This is normal for the species: the runt will not survive much longer. An uneaten lemming lay belly up among the willow twigs. His eyes were closed, and his little paws relaxed and were defenseless in death.

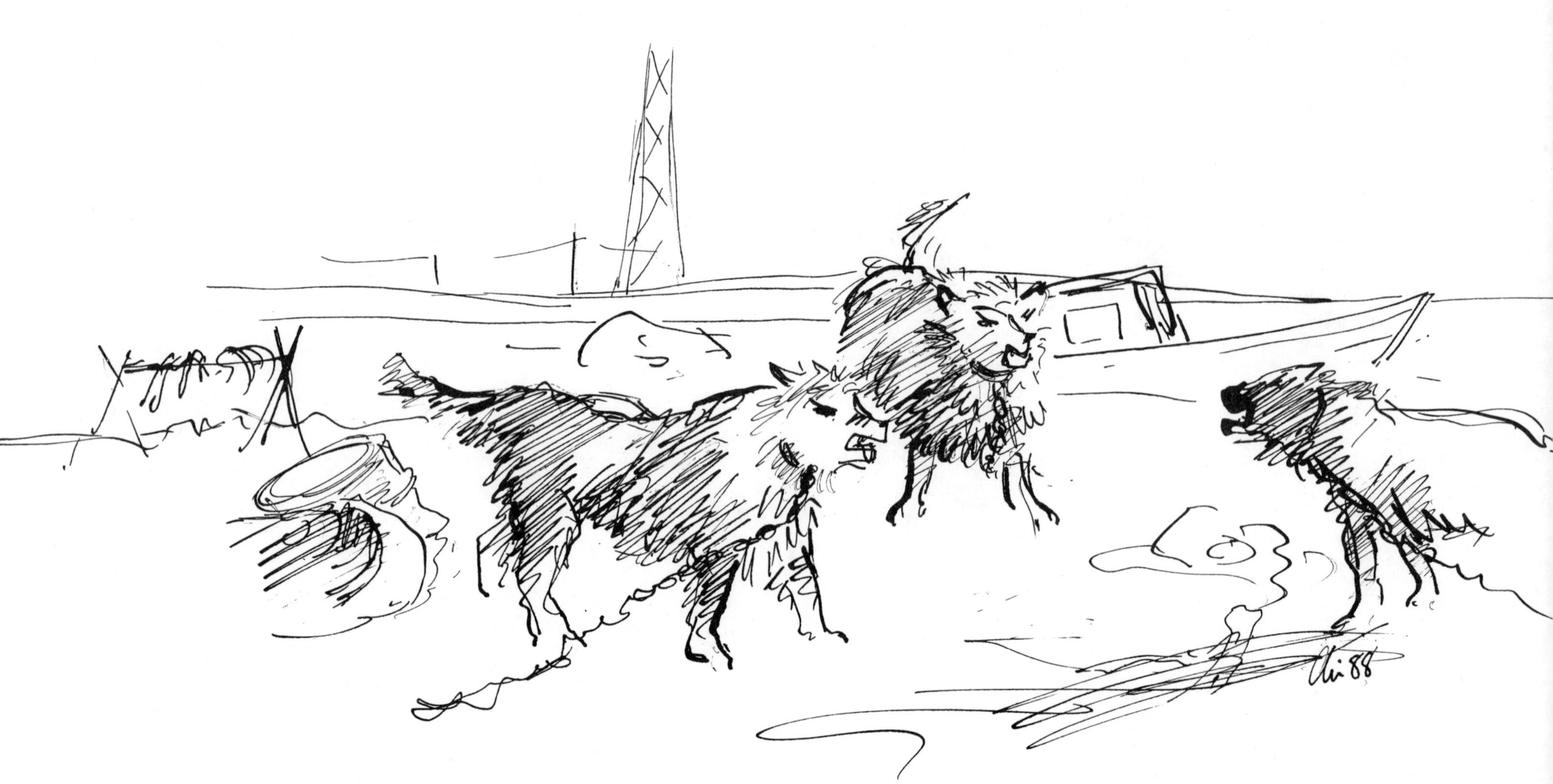

Steven Gray is the Anglican Minister at Cambridge Bay. Anyone less like the popular conception of a vicar could hardly be imagined, and I grew up in England, so I should know. Steven is a big, burly man with a Bronx accent and a fierce ginger beard. He chainsmokes and drinks great draughts of tea, Inuit fashion. He is one of the three men in the settlement to operate a dog team; what all the other dogs around town do, I have no idea. His wife is a quiet, elegant woman, an Indian from a reserve in Northern Quebec. They have adopted a local boy, and have a baby of their own.

Steven lives four doors down from Tomati, but, in the fashion of the town, I probably would not have done more than wave to him, and certainly not known who he was, had not Dennis and I met him while unloading stuff from the barge. Dennis had a trike and would have had to make several journeys with his groceries to his house, but Steven has a pickup, and he took everything for us in one load. We formed a human chain to throw the cases and boxes and sacks of flour up the steps into Dennis' porch. Then we went back with Steven to help him shift his groceries. The store in Edmonton had not packed the container well, and some of his cases of juice had been destroyed. No one takes responsibility for this, so Steven will have to foot the bill.

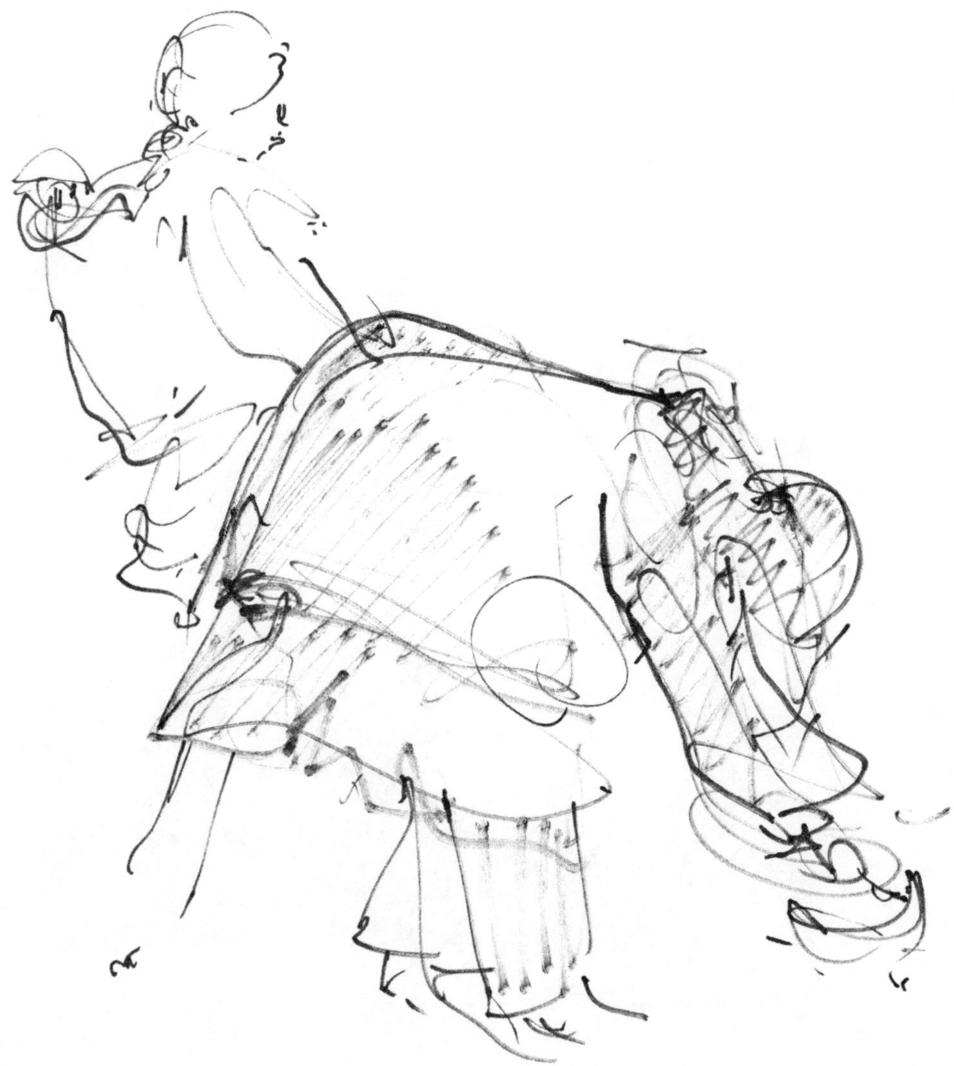

Steven's outer porch smelled of fish, and the deck of his truck was slimy with fish blood. That evening, he was driving out to his cabin at the West Arm fishing camp, and we went along for the ride, crouching in the open back, averting our faces from the wind.

The fishing camp, like everything else in this empty land, was stuck without ceremony upon it, and visible for miles. Many people, both white and Inuit, claim ownership of these wood and canvas shacks they call cabins. Some are used only at weekends, but some are lived in all summer, and those people who work in town commute. Steven's friends fished full time. Many of the older people had no use for the town and what it was doing to their young people. They preferred the old ways.

Like Tomati and Joseph, Steven's friends had anchored a net to the shore and spread it along the shallow shelf out to sea. Several times a day, they took a rowboat along the net and disentangled the heavy, silvery bodies. Steven, being white, was not allowed to fish with a net, but his wife, being native, had that right. Steven needed lots of fish to feed his dogs, so he provided the boat, and the Inuit caught enough fish for all of them. Hundreds of red-fleshed char hung on drying racks outside the cabins. Even though the Inuit have freezers, many still prefer the taste of dried fish.

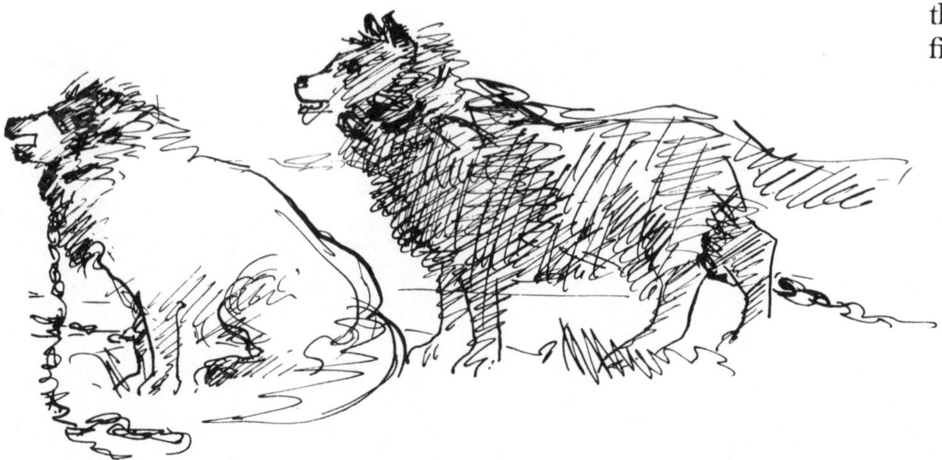

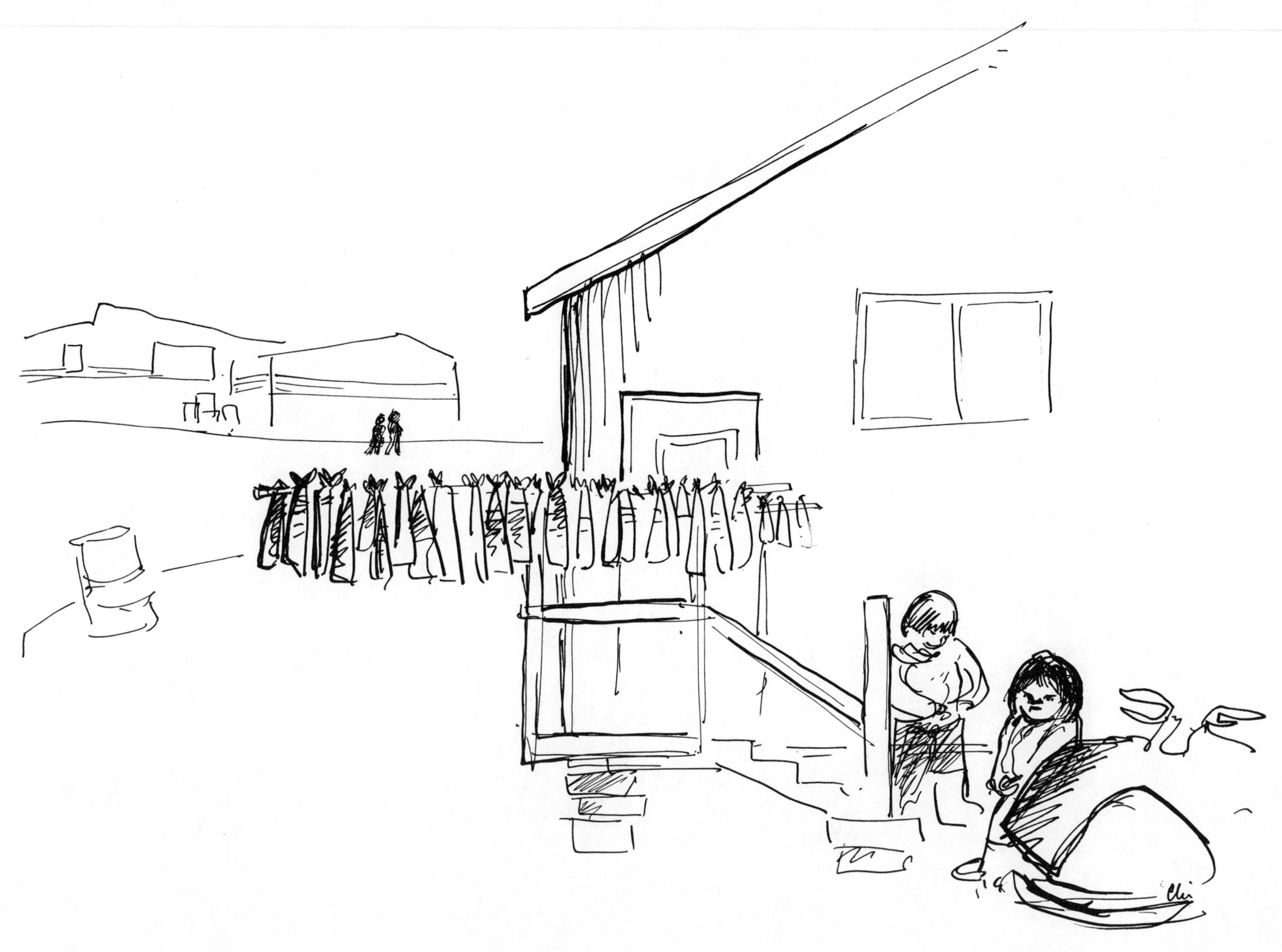

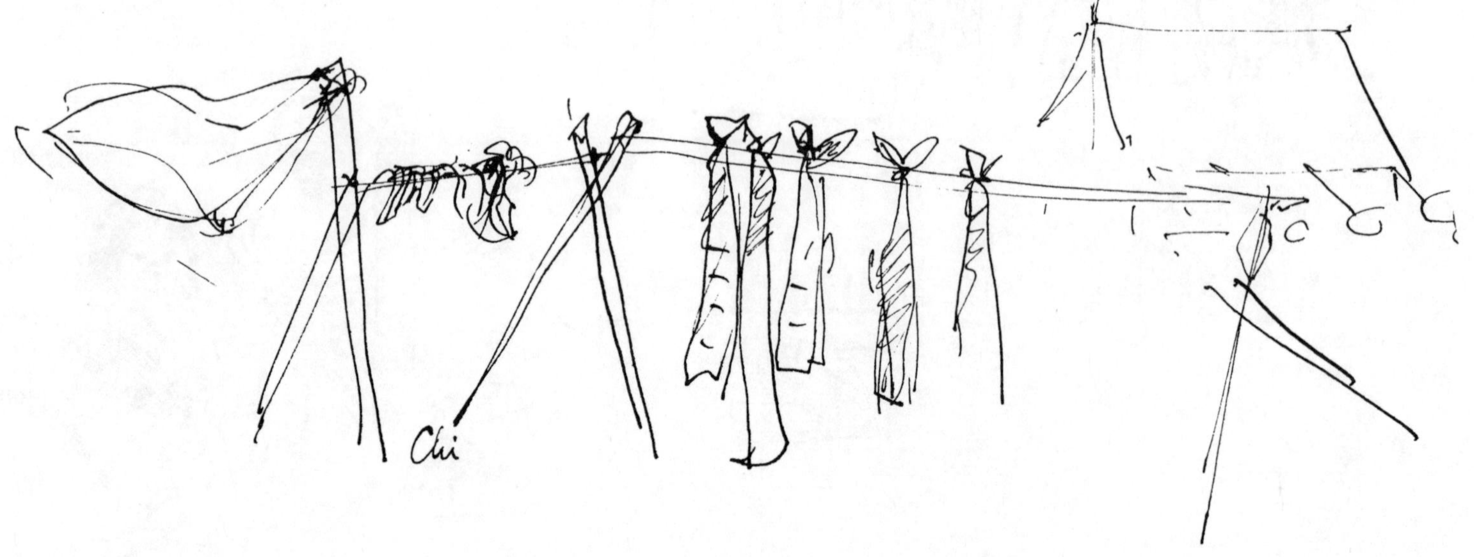

Steven's cabin was half wood, half canvas. It was businesslike inside, and very cozy, with a sleeping bench filling half of it and a small heater at one end. He pumped up the Coleman stove to make the inevitable tea. "This door is never locked," he said. "Nor are any of the doors around here. You can walk into these cabins anytime you want. You will always be welcome. If there is no one about, just help yourself to what you need. That's the way it is done here." These were people of the old ways.

It was, like the day when the icebreaker arrived, an evening of exceptional calm. The sun was a red ball; there was not a breath of wind. There was a nip of frost, and the sea was very still and luminous, heavy, like mercury, fired red gold by the long, low sun. It was very quiet. Tiny sounds, like the clink of stones, travelled far. The kids were throwing rocks into the water. Katie's slim blond boy is easily recognizable against the strong, brown, chunky bodies of the Inuit kids. He suffers sometimes, as children will, from this difference. But tonight he played happily with Steven's adopted child.

The sea was clear as glass: it breathed with the gentlest of movements. Small, strange jellyfish fluttered faintly close to shore. The kids discovered them and tried to bomb them. The stillness was disorientating.

It was dusk when we drove back to town. The icebreaker was in the bay, its red hull glowing with afterlight. The town and ship were all lights; windows, portholes, and rigging strung with lights like a Christmas tree. You could see the lights now it was dark enough. The reflections on the water were perfect. The ship floated above its mirror image, disembodied, hanging in a galaxy of lights.

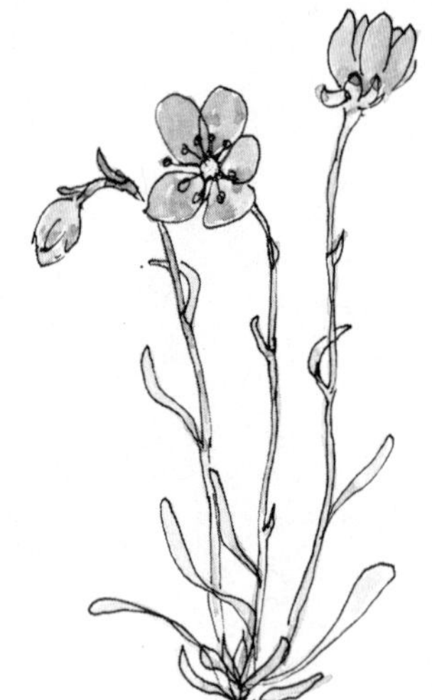

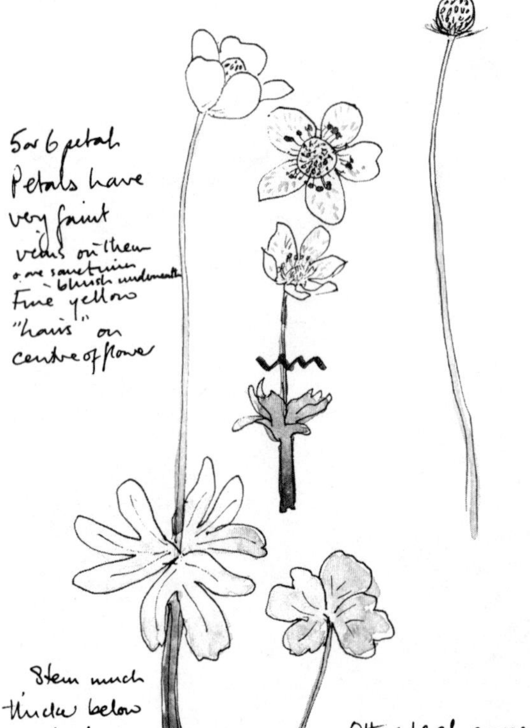

NORTHERN WINDFLOWER
SMALL FLOWERED WINDFLOWER
Anemone parviflora (Ranunculaceae)

5 or 6 petals
Petals have very faint veins on them — one sometimes bluish underneath
Fine yellow "hairs" on centre of flower

Stem much thicker below leaf.

Other leaf comes out of ground close by.

YELLOW MARSH SAXIFRAGE
Saxifraga hirculus

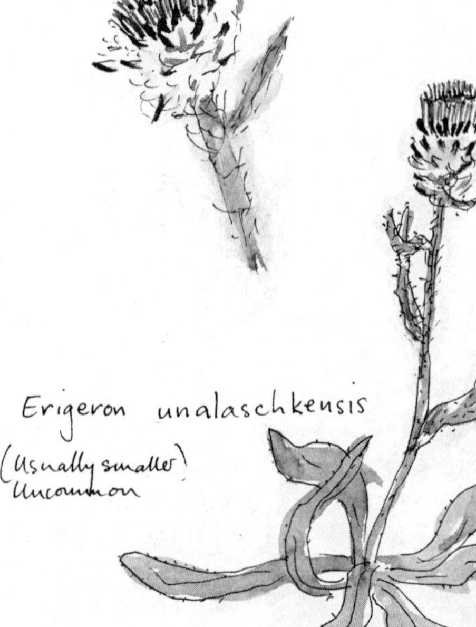

Sepals, stalks + upper leaves very hairy esp. sepals. Base leaves hairy only at edge.
Long Point.
Mid August.

Erigeron unalaschkensis

(Usually smaller)
Uncommon

1st September

I have collected ninety-five species of wild flowers. A team of German botanists has been camping near town, and they have identified them all for me. Like everyone else, the botanists are sick of the rain. Dietbert, the leader, has been to the Arctic often: he was so used to dry summers, he had not thought to bring decent rain gear with him. My own coat so old, it is about as much use as a paper bag in a downpour.

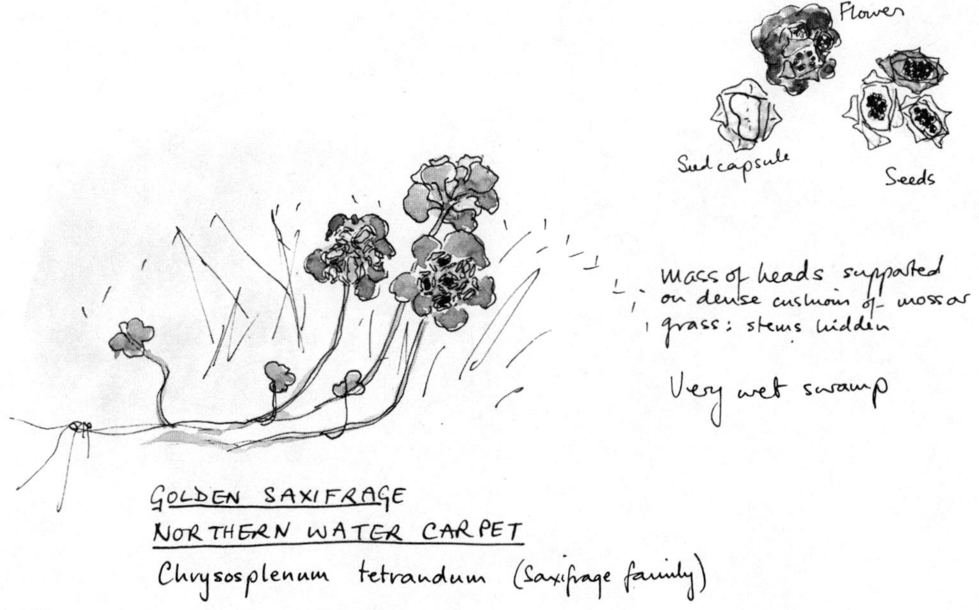

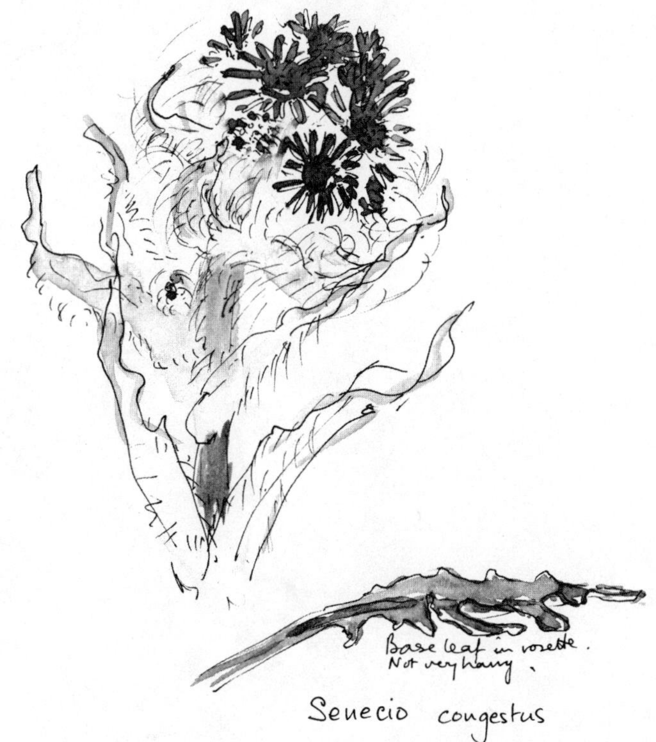

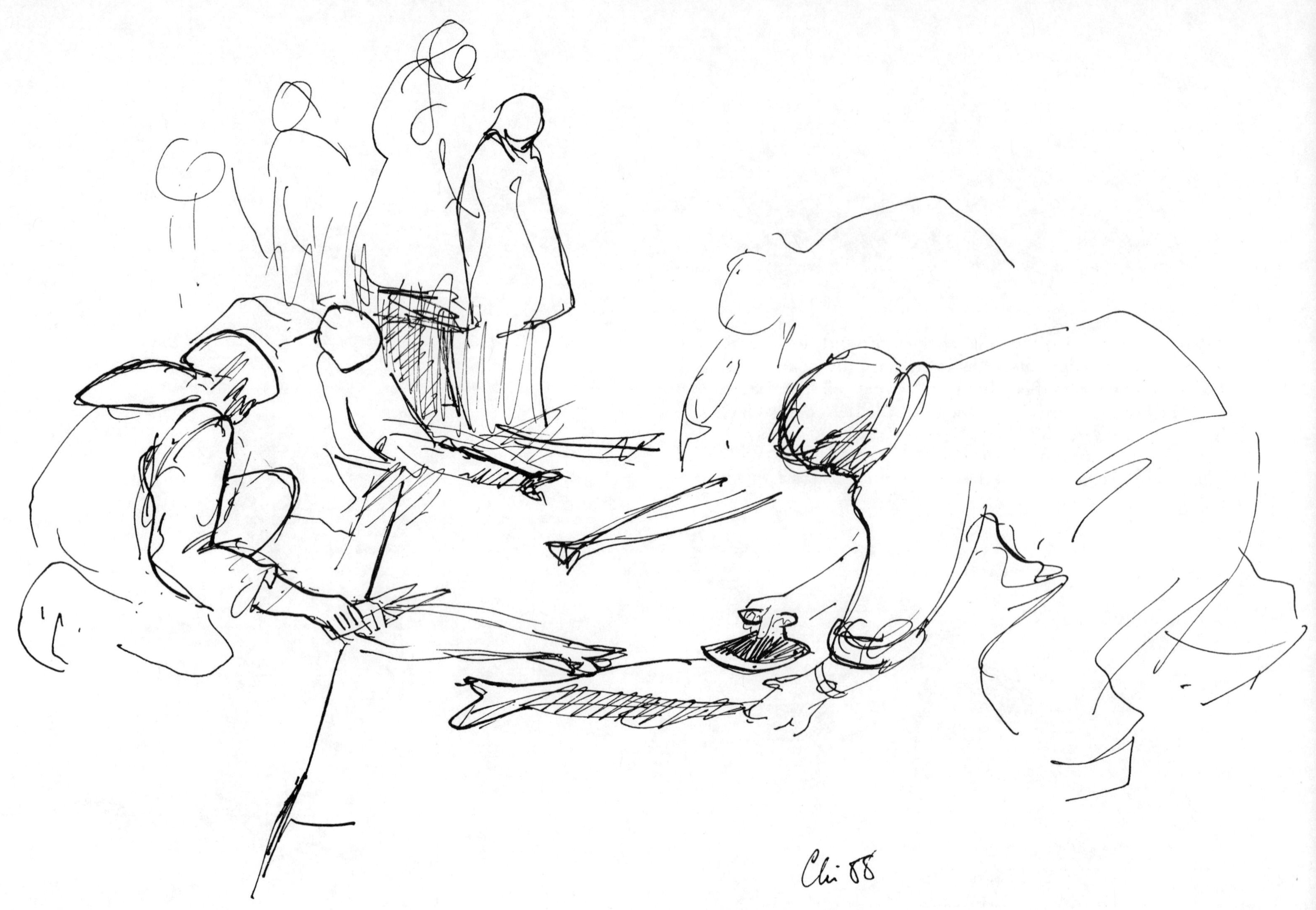

Dietbert is friends with a man, also a German, who runs the air charter service. The battered twin otter and beaver constantly roar across the bay from their base along the waterfront, and a wheeled executive jet operates from the runway at the airport. When there was a space on the plane, Dietbert sometimes went along for the ride. He told me he had seen the Belvedere, trapped by the long slab of ice between here and Pelly Bay. The Hobi Cat had managed to cross it, though, and they were far to the north, at the mouth of the Bellot Strait. We'd heard from air travellers to Pelly Bay that it had taken the boys nineteen days to cross the ice, dragging their boat, day after day. Now they were nearly through to the Atlantic, and it looked as though they would make it.

Dietbert hired a four-wheeled bike, and he invited me to go out with him one day to Long Point. The road, such as it is, fades out at the fishing camp at West Arm, but ATVs run along the gravel ridges then drop to the long, clean sweep of the sandy beach out to the point. I walked there often when I was camping, and it is a paradise for flowers: campions, thrifts, dwarf fireweeds, both white and red (the flower is identical to those which grow on the familiar tall spires that colonize a burn in the forests further south, but here it grows almost stalkless, in huge carpets, staining the tundra purple). There were many saxifrages, dandelions and a marvelously fuzzy Indian paintbrush, which has none of the brilliant reds and oranges of the south, but ranges from a plum colour to a pale cream. Few flowers would be blooming now, except the aggressive, straggling tansy mustard, which has the unusual distinction of being the only arctic plant to need man's interference with the soil before it can grow (it is thought to have come across the Bering land bridge with ancient waves of immigration from Asia), and the poppies, who don't know when to quit. The urge to procreate is so rigidly programmed, they simply keep on flowering until they freeze.

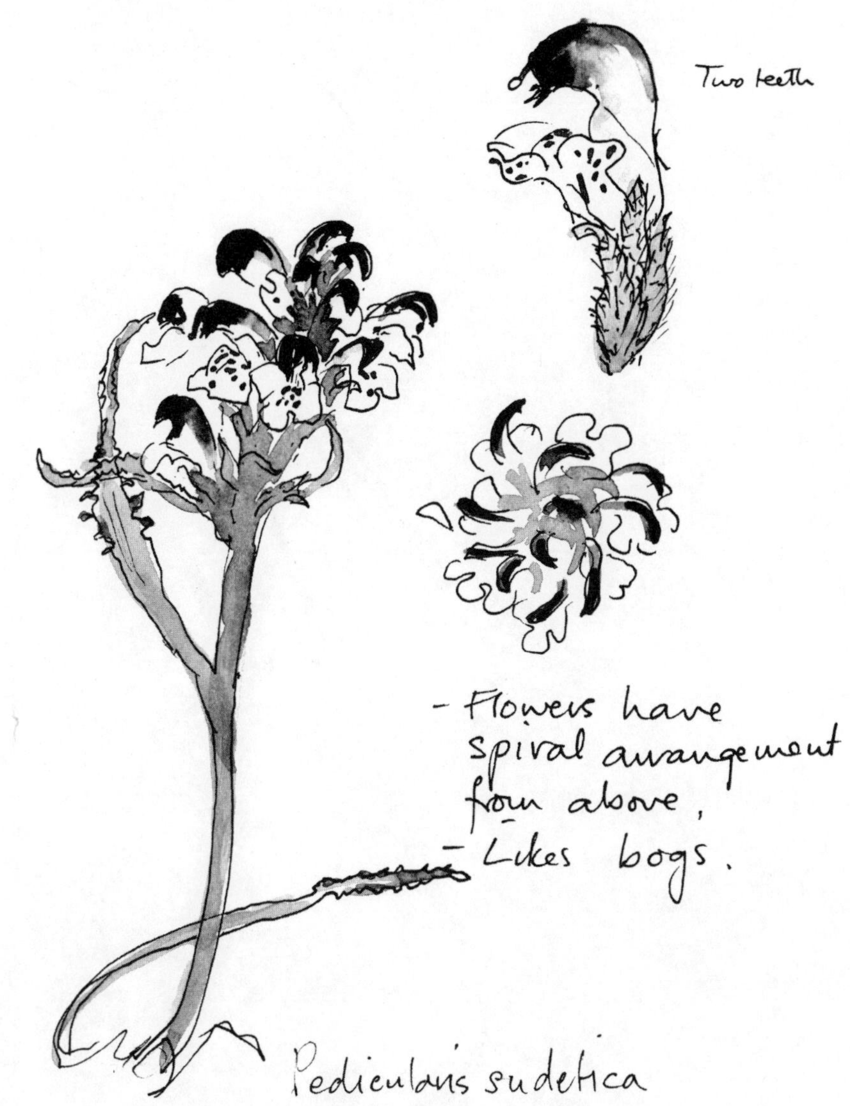

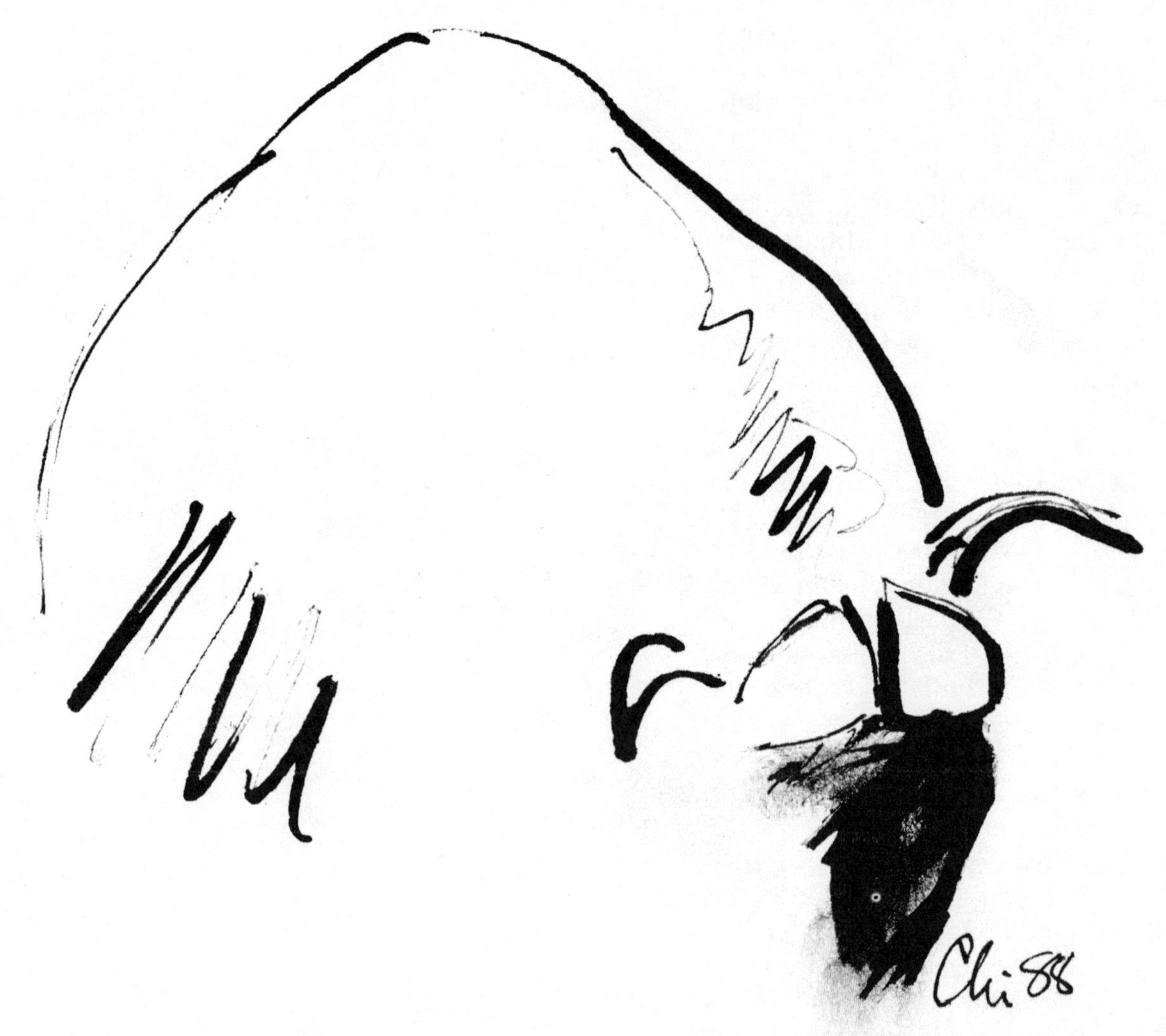

Beyond the point and its nearby hills, which are curious-
ly shaped as if they have been swept into heaps with a
broom, is an unusual topographical feature. A river has cut
a gorge for itself through a band of glacial sand and, on the
leeward side, steep sand cliffs have formed. Were it not for
the permafrost, they would have eroded long ago. I have
spent much time here, floundering in the shifting surface
soil, for many plants grow quite differently in this loose
shelter, and it was an endlessly fascinating place.

On the day I went with Dietbert, a wild day of vicious
squalls, the fall had come. The tundra was ablaze with
tiny, brilliant leaves, the yellow of the willow, and the wind
red of the bear berry. They lay like discarded jewels among
brittle lichens and the cushions of rich, green moss. There
were three muskox in the bottom of the gorge. When they
saw me, they galloped up the steep, loose slope as if it had
been level ground, and they stood on the rim, huffing and
blowing. The wind was particularly fierce there, and it
beat against our clothing and dragged and whipped the
animals' outer coats. These are coarse as horsetail and just
about as long. This bulk makes them look top-heavy; tiny
feet poke out underneath. "Oomingmak" means "Hairy
One." They have a gland on their forelegs, which they rub
with their heads when excited, and this gives them a look of
a bull about to charge. It is an instinctive threat behaviour,
and it sure works on me.

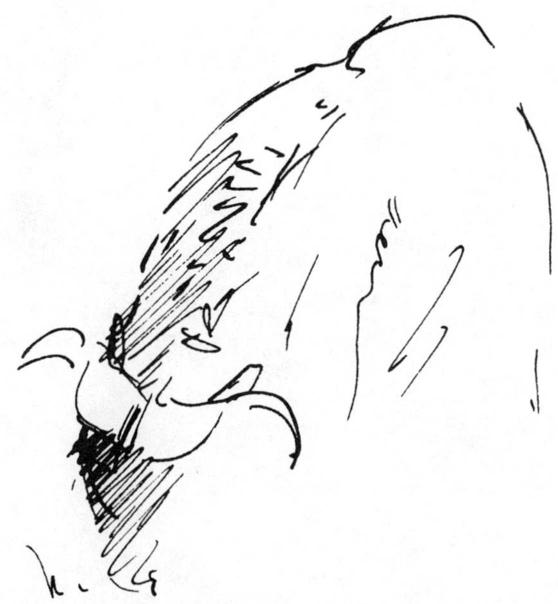

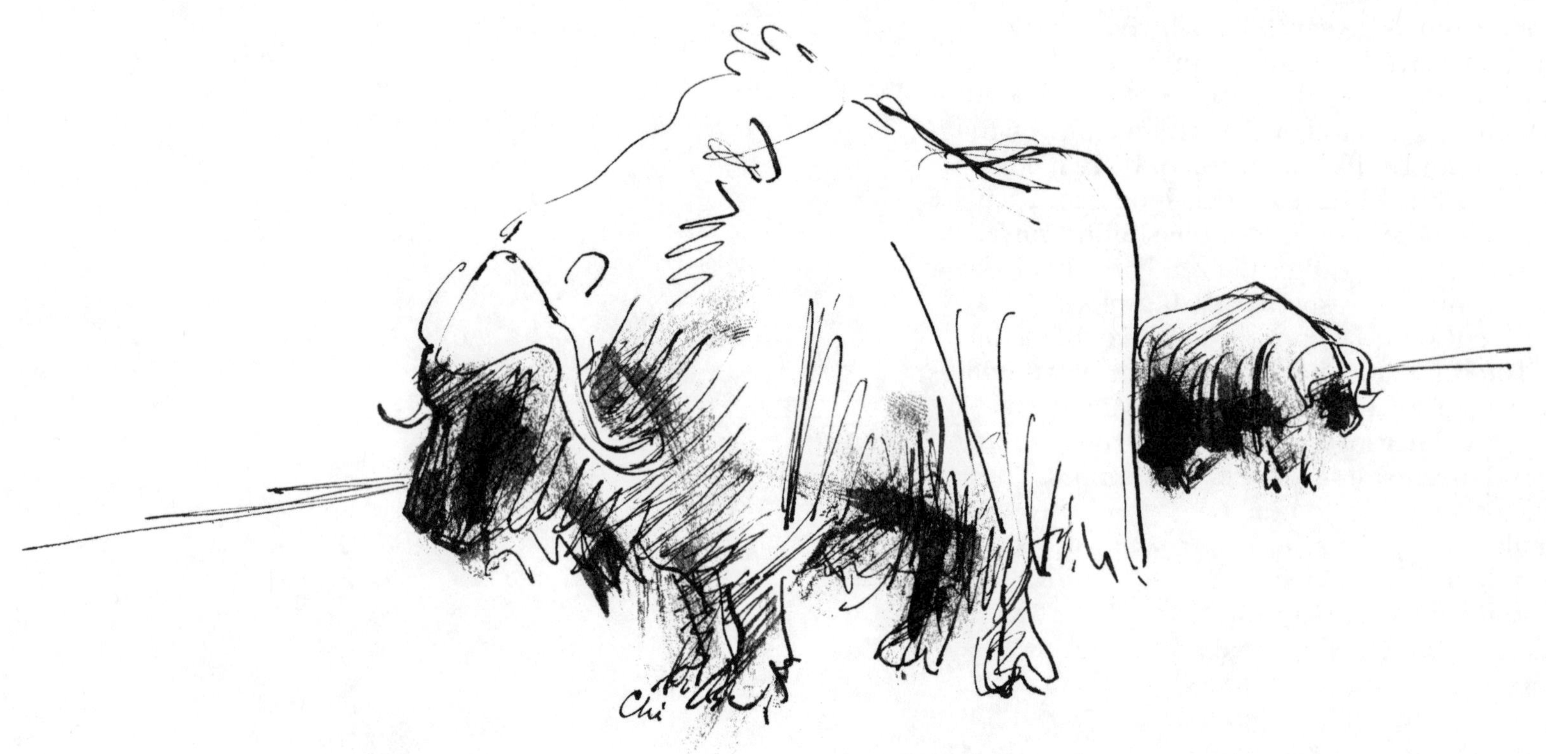

But Dietbert was not so cautious. He had encountered the Oomingmak too often to be afraid. He walked confidently forward. The beasts tossed their heads. I followed behind, reasoning that if they charged, Dietbert would be the one to get it first. I kept close to the rim of the canyon, ready to fling myself down it out of the way. Closer we grew, and closer. They threatened, we photographed. Soon, I had both Dietbert and the muskox within the frame of my viewfinder. If they did attack, I would have a wonderful action shot.

But nothing happened. The minute we began to withdraw, the animals lay down to chew their cud like cattle in a sunny field, eyes half closed, ears drooping contentedly, oblivious to the rain and wind. And we, weary of the ceaseless battering and cold, were envious of the Oomingmak. We turned for home.

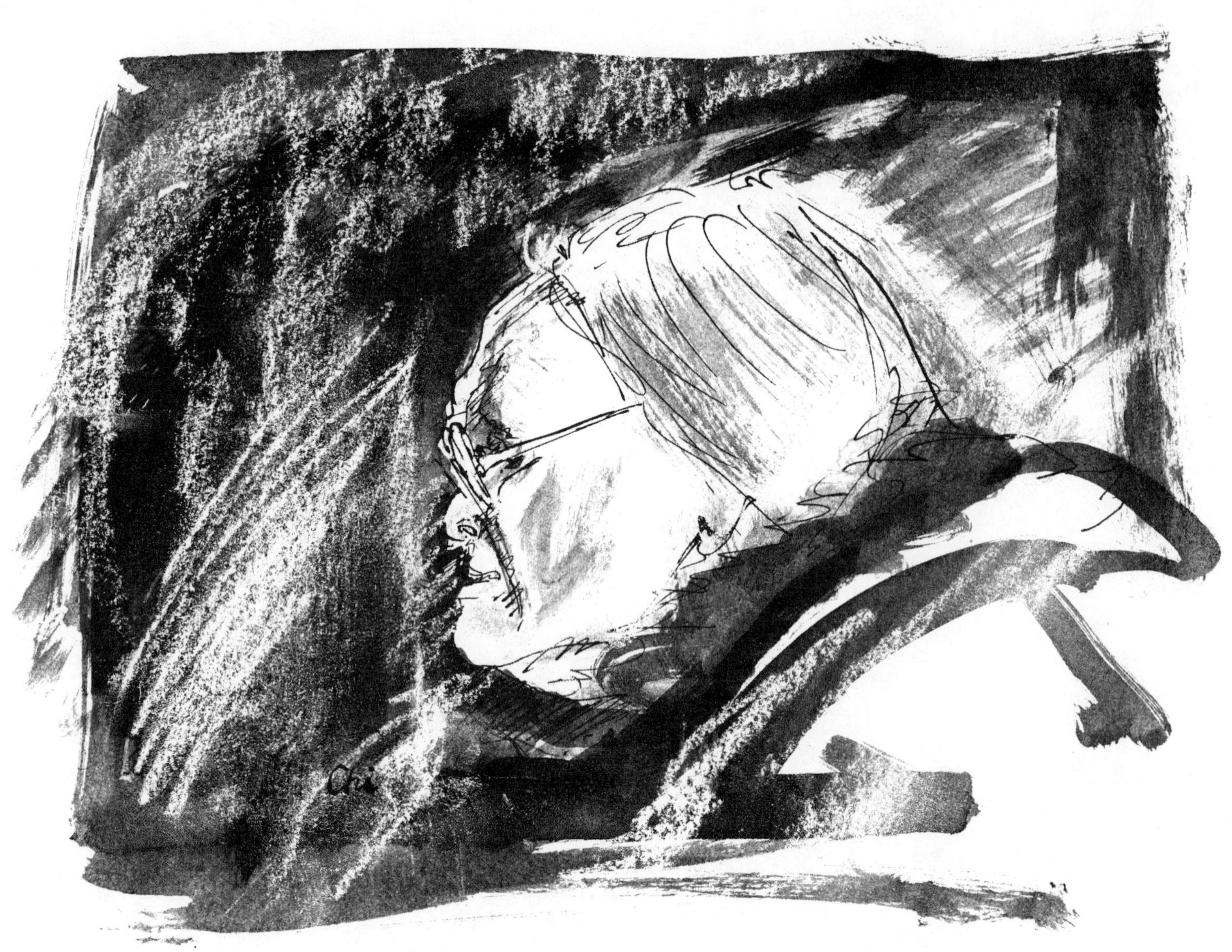

3rd September

My plane leaves at noon today, weather permitting. The temperature has dropped, and the ground froze in the bitter gales of yesterday. It snowed overnight. Whether it is still falling from the sky or simply stirred up by the wind is difficult to say. It drives across the tundra in horizontal sheets, scouring ridges, filling hollows, levelling the land. Stiff grass sticks through like the bristles on an old brush. In the two months I have been here, the land has swung through spring, summer, and fall; for the next ten months, it will be winter.

I walk along the road to Mt. Pelly. I progress slowly, leaning, trudging, with one arm shielding the edge of my face, and frequently I turn my head away to breathe. The frozen ruts on the road are filling with a wind-smoothed snow as fine as flour. The tundra is disappearing. The papery petalled poppies, blooming till the last, are frozen on their stalks, and snow piles up against them. It is hard to realize that at home the world is somnolent with summer, and the gardens will be rich and lush with vegetables. That will be something to look forward to, at any rate. All fresh produce must be flown up here from California, and it is pretty old and sometimes frost damaged when it arrives. I bought an apple from the store the other day for a dollar and thirty cents.

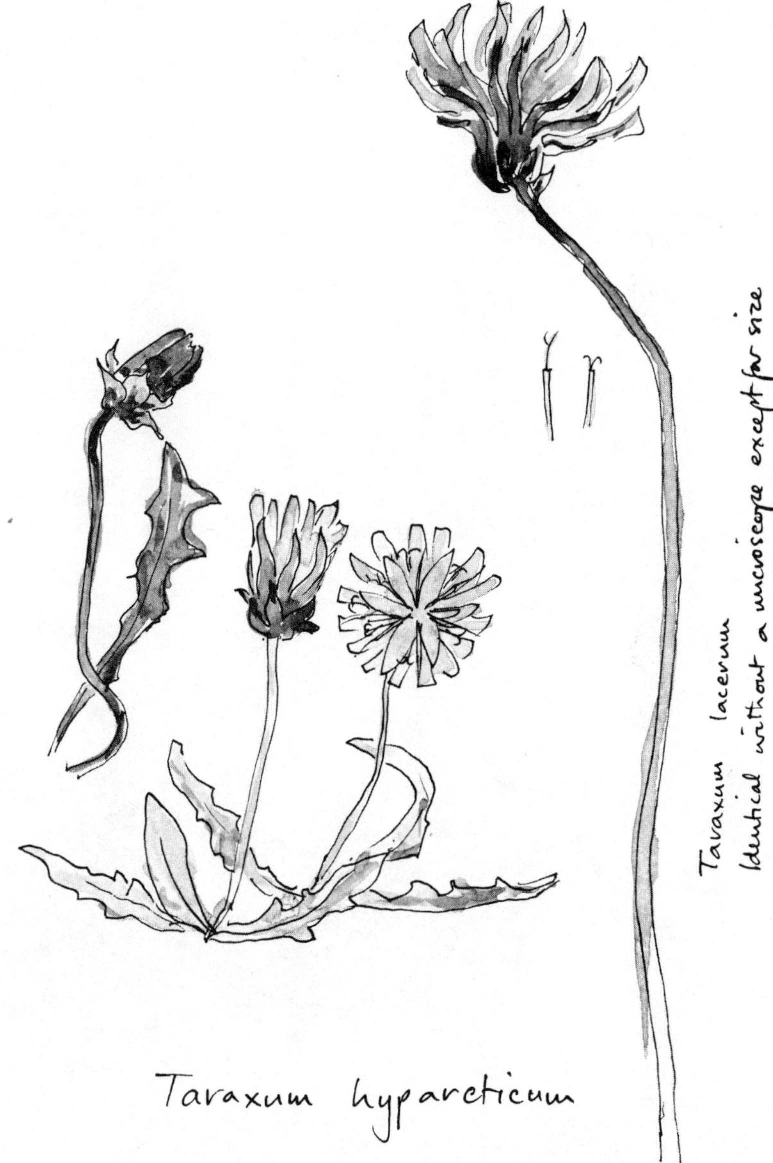

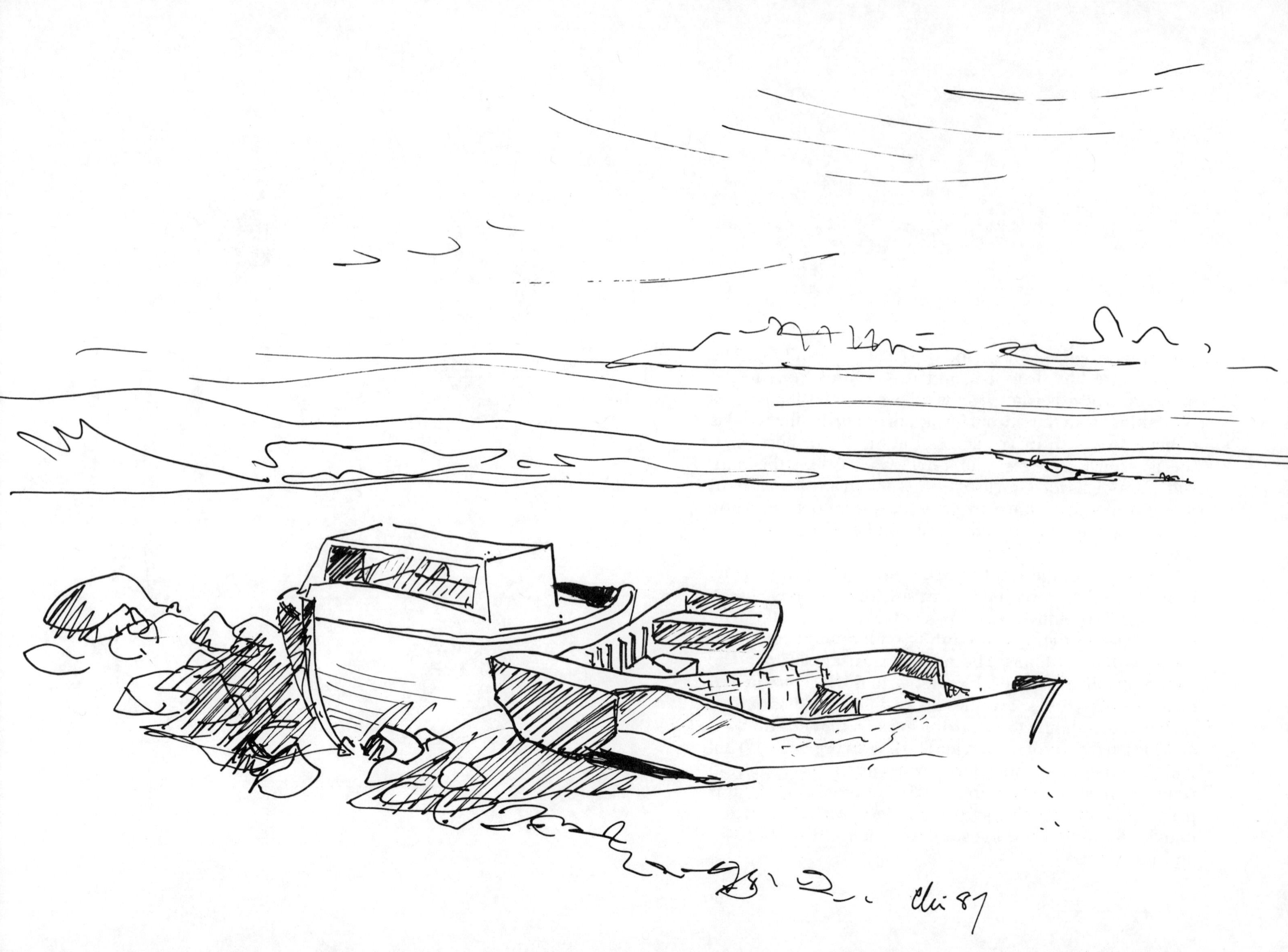

I turn back to town and freeze the other side of my face. In the gravel pit, a bulldozer driver is working, grinding his rattling machine. White or native, I do not know: I cannot see his face. He waves automatically, curious about this much belated tourist; all the others have long gone — flown south, with the geese. He swings his machine around, and turns his back to me. Work is work. Wind, sun, rain or snow, it is all the same to him.

The great sea
Has set me adrift
It moves me as a weed in a great river.
Earth and the great weather
Move me
Have carried me away
And move my inward parts with joy

Uranuk, a woman Shaman of the Igloolik Eskimos.
Quoted by Knud Rasmussen.

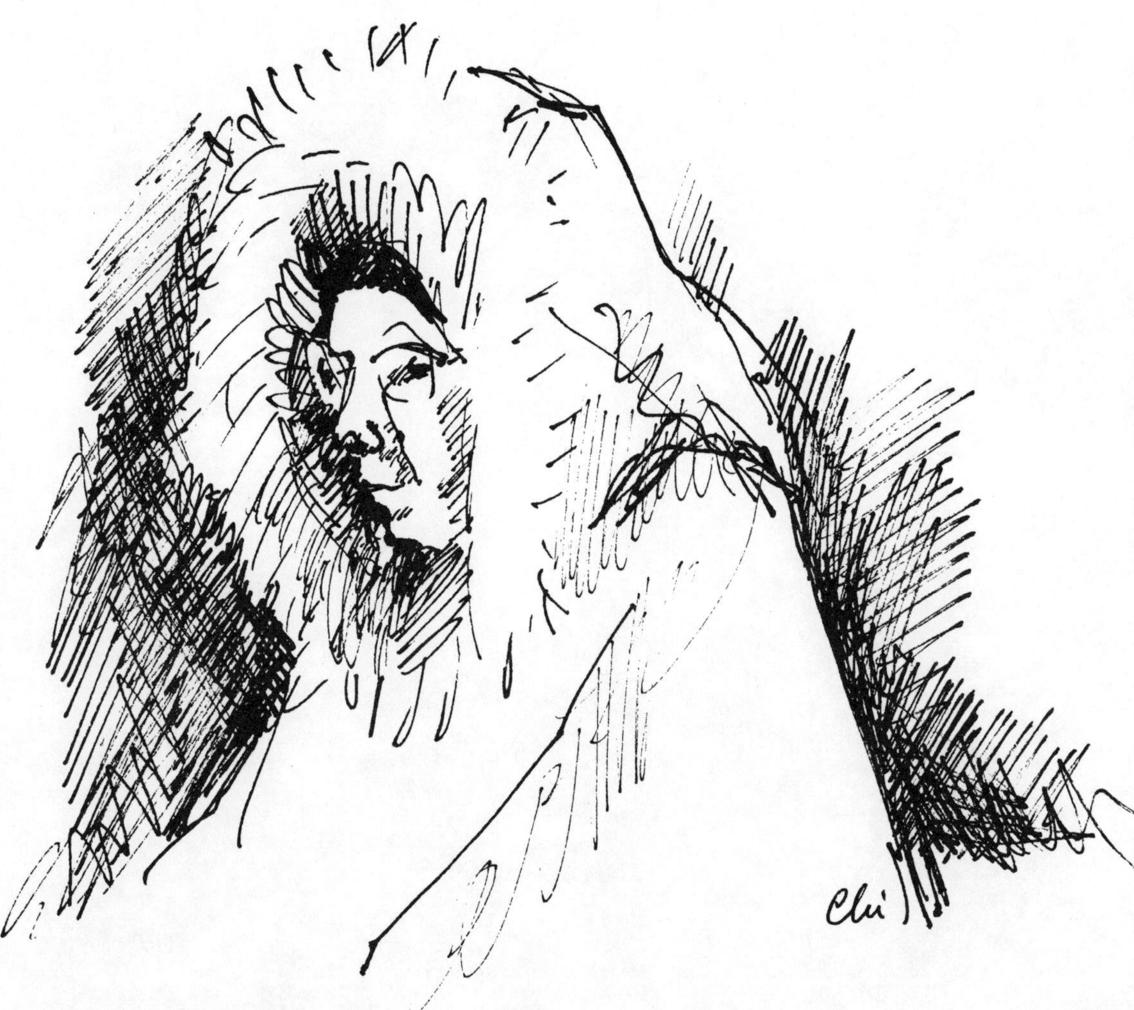